"Today's children – more than ever in the history of mankind – need guidance. ❧ That guidance that is pure and wonderful, that can only come from the energy, that wondrous energy, that you call God. ❧ If mankind realised the impact that these wonderful lessons have for every man, woman and child wherever they may be, then the peace that you hold so dear to your hearts would descend upon this magical planet called Earth."

God bless,
Spirit.

Previously published by:
SPIRITUAL PHILOSOPHY PUBLISHING LIMITED

SOME SILENT HERO
MAITREYA VOLUME ONE

Coming Soon

THE CHIEF'S FORGOTTEN LAND
MAITREYA VOLUME TWO

Secrets from the Universe

– Volume 1 –

Stepping Stones

Inspirational Writings

Désirée Jestico

Spiritual Philosophy Publishing Limited

"Stepping Stones":
Secrets from the Universe.

Published in 2006 by:
Spiritual Philosophy Publishing Limited
PO Box 79
Midhurst
West Sussex
GU29 9WW

Spiritual Philosophy Publishing website:
www.spiritualphilosophy.co.uk

British Library Cataloguing in Publication Data.
A catalogue record for this book is available
from the British Library.

ISBN 10 : 0-9548959-2-4

ISBN 13 : 978-095489592-1

Printed and bound by Cambridge University Press.
Book Design and Typesetting by Cecil Smith.
Set in New Baskerville
Cover Design by Ian Tyrrell of RPM, Chichester.

The publisher wishes to thank every individual and company
that has helped put this book into print.

Contents

Acknowledgement

To receive these readings from the World of Spirit is one thing, but to offer them in an acceptable form for the publisher is quite another.

I could not have done this without the valuable help and encouragement from Yve Cattermole. Although she has a family and a full time job, it is through her computer expertise, time and energy that this timeless book is now available to all. To her I shall be ever grateful.

Foreword

Once in a while, someone stands up to be counted and in so doing, the help millions receive is colossal.

This book does that job and comes at a time when mankind is asking more questions than ever about the meaning of life.

Through her inspirational writings Désirée keeps compassion to the fore and her work can offend no religion; simply because it is a book on how mankind can help itself.

Wander through the pages at your leisure or in times of strife. In so doing, your centre of wisdom will be prodded and awakened by the things you already knew, but had forgotten with the pressure of multiple choice and the excessive demands of western living. Each and every one of us is a walking book on how it is.

Locate that wisdom again – with Désirée's help – and live this glorious gift called life to the full.

Meg Pringle Adamson.

Introduction

These short readings are intended for either public or private use. They can also be used for personal reflection, leading to a deeper understanding of the Universal Truth of Life. The statements made throughout the book retell the age-old themes in a different way; sometimes a better understanding is achieved because the ideas are turned around.

I have received these words through inspiration in quiet times. At first these words of deeper truth were unsought, but realising their significance, I willingly sat quietly allowing my mind to be filled with these lovely words. I was aware that such statements have been made throughout the ages but often it is the way they are expressed that will appeal to many.

Each one has been read in public and the response was amazing. It is as though there is a deep hunger for words such as these. They will offer comfort to many and give focus for meditation for those who need to go deeper in understanding.

When life seems to be going well, many feel they can go it alone without asking for spiritual guidance. It is as well to keep in mind that we all visit this planet Earth to learn in order to progress toward ultimate perfection. Often the lessons are hard indeed, but without the support of those in Spirit we would find life almost impossible.

Daily inspiration can be found by opening this book at random and using the words found as a friend; to offer help and comfort through the darkest hours of experience. Some lonely souls are in search of happiness. This elusive quality will not be found in the acquisition of wealth and possessions. One has to realise that happiness for one person would not necessarily be happiness for another. Helping others before personal consideration will prove to be the key to the unlocking of many of life's mysteries – even happiness.

Keep your dreams and aspirations and find your true pathway through the pages of this book.

Désirée Jestico

NB – Permission is NOT required of the Publisher or Author to read these teachings to an audience, whether in public or in private.

Reading a Verse at a Gathering:

Every day, someone, somewhere reads an inspirational message in a Church, School, Conference or just a gathering of like-minded people. Whether or not the message gets over to the audience *and* is a success depends totally on the preparation, explanation and delivery of the reading. Here are a few pointers:

- Read through the Verse several times – get comfortable with the message
- Find *all* the points of emphasis
- Mark the points where you need to rest, so that the audience can absorb what has been said up to that point
- Don't rush – take your time
- Explain any unusual words *before* the text is delivered
- Always give your reading with Love
- Enjoy the reading yourself and the audience will warm to you
- Make it fun if you can
- Finally, always – but always – introduce the reading, tell the audience what the reading is about and set the scene.

Setting the Scene:

The following introduction is merely a suggestion as to how to tell the gathering about the Verse to follow. Often, Inspirational Writings use a form of language that is somewhat 'old fashioned.' Words are often spoken in traditional English grammatical form and not in the colloquial idiom of the day. If a reading is going to touch the hearts of the audience, the individual personality of the reader must come through; hence the following is but one suggestion:

This refers to Verse 2:

'While we tend to focus on the fact that we are 'human beings' with assorted body shapes, different coloured skins and different languages, today's teaching emphasises that we are all primarily just souls on a journey. We are here on the Earth Plane to learn lessons before we go back to the World of Spirit or Heaven as we know it. There are several writings that have identified the 'Hall of Mirrors' as the place that we are shown to when we undertake our 'Life Review.' This Verse is a wonderful insight into the process we will all go through, when we first arrive in Heaven.'

Now read Verse 2:

> *"We have spoken about the next step that you all face after leaving your World of Matter. You will all have a wonderful welcome…*

After the reading you may want to add a few words:

"This reading has been a wonderful opportunity for us all to remember that our main purpose in life is to spread love in the world. It is a 'wake-up' call for change in our lives – hopefully changes for the better – God bless.'

Verses: 1 to 142

The following verses are part
of a library of over 400 inspirational writings
given over a 10 year period.
The verses in this book span a period from
1st January 1996 to 27th May 2001.

Verse 1

Themes:

- Contact with Spirit
- Life after Death
- Love
- Mediumship

"To bring you evidence that life continues after 'apparent' death, there must be no doubt in your mind that contact is established with your loved one. ~ The only way that this can be done is for your loved one to show the condition and the feeling that brought them to the Spirit World. ~ Do not feel upset when the pain and the distress at the end of the physical life is shown or described. ~ We want to assure each one here, that whatever was the suffering, it can no longer affect them. ~ It is the memory that is brought forward when Earth contact is made and intended only for identification; the pain is no longer real. ~ For some, who did not suffer pain or distress, the mode of dress or some particular mannerism will ensure recognition. ~ These are only memories, which are used to prove that your loved one still lives and is only a thought away. ~ The body that you use in the Spirit World is an exact replica of your earthly body when it was young, fit and well. ~ In fact, it is not necessary to own a body that looks like an Earth body, but until there is advanced understanding it is of great help to those in the lower planes. You do not need legs in order to move. ~ You do not need a head and face in order to speak. ~ *All* activity comes from the mind. ~ It is your thoughts, your experience and understanding, and the way that these are used that govern your progress through the Spirit Planes. ~ We find it pleasant and comfortable to have an earth-like body and to see others in the conventional way, but in reality it is not necessary. ~ We have been told that the further one progresses, the less and less the body is even thought of as pleasant! ~ Eventually, at some far point in eternity, we shall all become light. ~ The prospect is so distant that we cannot understand what it means. ~ We *do know* that all progress is gradual and evolving, with no sudden dramatic changes, and *all* is an expression of love. ~ Love is the vehicle of all progress toward the Godhead."

Verse 2

Themes:
- Judgment
- Karma
- Life Review*
- What happens when we die?

"We have spoken about the next step that you all face after leaving your World of Matter. ~ You will all have a wonderful welcome that each newcomer receives on arrival in our world; it is a welcome home after the Earth adventure. ~ Now the next important experience is about to begin; it is the complete review of your life on the Earth Plane. ~ Unless this review is undertaken, there can be no progress. ~ In some ways it is like watching a film on Earth but instead of some famous film star, the 'star' so called, is *you*. ~ The film you see is the minute detail of all your life; all your thoughts and actions, but more importantly, how those thoughts and actions affected others. ~ Most of this detail you would have forgotten, but this re-run will bring it all back with such clarity that your interest will be held in amazed fascination. ~ It is the sudden realization that the thought that led to the action, and the affect on others and *their* subsequent thoughts, that bring you up sharply. ~ It is this greater sense of awareness that causes remorse for wrong actions to well up within you. ~ You wish you had known and realized while on the Earth Plane. ~ You are living your life again with all the feelings that accompanied the experience, but you also plumb the depths of the feelings of others. ~ The most valuable experience of all through this,

* Life Review: When we pass over into the World of Spirit, we undertake a review of the life that we have lead as described above. Other inspirational writings tell us that it takes place in the Hall of Mirrors.
Note: Conventional religious thought posits that we are judged when we go to Heaven. Since we are all a spark of God, Spirit tells us that we actually judge ourselves.

are the feelings you have while you watch. ~ In some scenes you may despise yourself for the pettiness that it exposes. ~ In other scenes you may be surprised and pleased at the effect your action has had for the better. ~ We will underline here one important point, **all the while you are judging yourself**. ~ The feelings are often overwhelming, but they will set the tone of your next step on the road of progress. ~ We urge you to watch your thinking and your subsequent actions. ~ Think kindly of others and help where you are able, so that when your review comes it will not cause you too much distress. ~ Remember too that Love *does* conquer all things."

Verse 3

Themes:

Healing · Life in Spirit · Love · Service

"All who speak to you from our World have told you that we have no night. ~ Ours is eternal day, for we have no need for sleep as you do. ~ We *do* rest, not because we are tired, but when we feel the need of a change of activity. ~ Our resting is often just a period to appreciate the fullness of the beauty that is always around us. ~ We may wish to walk through one of the many beautiful gardens created for all to enjoy, or to contemplate the journey of the water as it laughs and chatters its way downstream. ~ Our wonderful light, which makes the water sparkle on its way, is brighter than your sunlight but is of a different quality. ~ It is a glowing radiance which cannot be identified as from a particular source. ~ The glow is not only warm, as is your Sun, but it is the glow and radiance of love and comes from every direction. ~ When we asked why we could not see the source as you can – and know it is your Sun – we were told that the radiance is from the Godhead and the Higher Beings that are close to the Godhead. ~ These wonderful Beings have progressed so far in advance, and their inner light has grown so great that it extends far beyond what was once their Spirit Body. ❧ They give out this wonderful light, which is also pure love. ❧ When we rest, we contemplate all these things and consciously bathe in their all-encompassing love. ❧ This is how we renew ourselves. ❧ You also have an inner light, which will grow brighter as you give service and love to others. ❧ The love that you give can be healing thoughts to the many throughout your World who are in need of the healing energy. ❧ You may never know how others benefit, but those in our World gather these thoughts of healing and take them to the needy. ❧ It is not the spectacular gifts of service that are needed but the continuous moments of love for others."

Verse 4

Themes:
- Healing
- Helping Others
- Living a Spiritual Life
- Meditation

"Living on the Earth Plane becomes a series of habits. ❧ The human soul likes the familiarity and comfort of ritual. ❧ We can so easily understand this, as once we were living on the Earth Plane too. ❧ If life was to be *really* different every day it would cause great unhappiness, as no-one would know what to expect; and the unsettling aspect of day to day living would become a burden. ❧ So the familiar and normal patterns of thinking are the base of most lives. ❧ What we want you to do is to bring to the fore in *your* mind, that life and living is forever. ❧ Once this fact is totally absorbed, we want you to form habits of thinking and acting as a background in your life. ❧ We know that many of you do set aside a few minutes each day in which to be still and meditate. ❧ It is so important, but we want you to make it a habit. ❧ Once it is a habit you will realize how important a habit it has become. ❧ Many of you will have your own absent healing list; you may not look on it as such, but most days you will remember your family who are sick as well as your friends. ~ Perhaps you pray for them or specifically ask for healing. ~ There are also the occasions when you see some people are hurt or who have suddenly been sent to our World. ~ When you hear about it or see it on television, you find a feeling of compassion rise up within you. ~ At such times, healing is sent on your behalf by the healers in our World. ~ These are all wonderful habits to get into. ~ Make it a habit too of sending a blessing to all who are disabled when you see them during your days – to cultivate habits such as these will make your life a blessing to all those around you. ~ It is at no cost to you individually, and all in all, so little time is spent on this habit activity as we have outlined. ~ While you live on the Earth you do not realize the extent of the good that will result, but when you come home you will find you will reap a far greater harvest than you had sown."

Verse 5

Themes:

Judging people · Not interfering with other peoples lives · Religion · Spiritual Movement

---

"There are many people who would prevent you from taking any part in this belief you call Spiritualism. ~ In most cases it is fear which drives them to attack those who believe in eternal life. ~ Deep within they know that what we say is true, but are afraid that by admitting it, *their* world will be in ruins. ~ They know within themselves that what we bring is truth and knowledge, but feel they must attack this belief in order to protect all that has been built up over the years by *their* leaders. ~ In most cases it is the blind leading the blind. ~ They say you should allow the 'dead' to rest in peace, but we can assure you that the 'dead' are very much alive. ~ They are more alive in our world than ever they were on the Earth Plane. ~ These 'dead' people want to make contact with their families and friends to assure them that the body of matter that was buried is of no further use to them. ❧ The stories of rising up at the last trump are examples of a vivid imagination, designed as a sop to an otherwise grim story of hell-fire and damnation *if* the bidding of *their* leaders was not followed. ❧ These graphic pictures of punishment were intended to keep control over their congregations. ❧ There is a state of Hell – as we have said at another time – but it is entirely a state of one's own making. ❧ Again, it is often stated that as you sow, so shall you reap. ❧ If you think about it, it is not unreasonable. ❧ No-one is condemned to anything. ❧ Those who try to prevent others from acquiring knowledge of our world are sowing the seeds from which they will not want the harvest when they return home to our world. ❧ We urge you to think of your actions and let love flow through your life. ❧ Pray for those misguided souls, that one day soon, they will begin to understand that this wonderful knowledge that we bring, will spread through every country; bringing freedom from the restrictions of organised religions and that no more, will killing take place in the name of the Godhead."

Verse 6

Themes:

Beauty · Choices · Discernment · Wisdom

"There is a saying of the Earth Plane which states that: 'Beauty is in the eye of the beholder.' ❧ This is certainly true but it must depend on how the beholder sees beauty. ❧ If the beholder is caught off guard by a pretty covering alone, then disappointment will soon take over. ❧ Those who find gaudy things attractive can never understand others who are more cautious and want to dig further to find what is really there. There are some Earth festivals which seem to encourage shopkeepers to display 'gaudy rubbish' to beguile those who are easily taken in by such things. ❧ There may be some people whom you meet who are *not* what they pretend to be; the pretty dress or smart suit may turn your thoughts in the wrong direction. ❧ Delve beneath the surface before – too quickly – accepting what is on offer. ❧ Throughout life on the Earth Plane you will find many traps for the unwary, but the wise will be able to find a way round them. ❧ For this reason we urge you to start your day, every day, asking for protection and guidance for the day ahead. ❧ Ask too, that love from the Godhead will surround you and lead you forward. ❧ You may still face difficulties, but they are part of life's lessons and experiences that all must face. ❧ If the path seems harder than usual, pause for a moment and renew the prayer for guidance that you invoked that morning. ❧ In this way you will understand the closeness of Spirit at all times, even when the next step seems impossible. ❧ You only need to ask and those in Spirit will help where they can. ❧ Not every day will test you, and some days will be sweetness itself; but look around and you will see the deeper meaning of life. ❧ You will not be tempted by the outer, but will find the inner beauty in all things. ❧ Allow your *own* wisdom to guide you and help you to see the inner qualities of the people you meet. ❧ Do not be distracted by any outer covering but keep the 'light of truth' by your side. ❧ The true beholding of beauty is the inner wisdom shining through. ❧ Let love guide you throughout your life and you will be a centre for peace and contentment."

Verse 7

Themes:
Advanced Meditation · Balance in Life · Prayer

"When you go into the silence for a period of meditation, do you just try to empty your mind for a few minutes then say a few prayers of healing and finish? ❧ We hope your meditation period is far more valuable than that. ❧ It should be a time that is considered precious; because it is *then* that you are really close to the World of Spirit. ~ We want you to shut out all the Material World and its activities. ~ It is for this reason that we advise you to ensure that your precious time is free from interruptions, as far as you are able to do it. ~ Gentle, deep breathing will lift your vibrations to a more acceptable level for us to draw very close. ~ It is then that we can give you the help that you may have requested, or to give you the knowledge that you have been seeking. ~ It is not a one-way traffic only; you must do your part too. ~ When you have stilled your mind as far as is within reason – we do not ask you to think of nothing – you will feel yourself being led. ~ At this point you may actually see where you are being taken. ~ If you cannot see, then the feeling of being led will help your imagination to visualize the journey. ~ This is where visualisation can be so helpful; for quite without you realizing it, your Spirit Helpers will take over and then you will actually see. ~ However it is done, you will be conscious of a movement during which you will receive the answers you have mentally posed. ~ You may not succeed – as we have outlined – the first time you try to do this, but with patience and the will to succeed, you will achieve a much more rewarding period of meditation than you have experienced until now. ~ When you do find success you will tend to get caught up with it, perhaps to the detriment of your worldly duties. ~ If this does happen, you will need to be firm with yourself and limit your meditation activity. ~ **The whole success of a happy Earth life is the balance between the material and the spiritual.** ~ Too much of one will cause an imbalance and sickness will be the result. ~ Your spiritual life will benefit from a well ordered material life and your material life will benefit from a carefully placed spiritual dimension. ~ During all your efforts, remember that a desire to be of service to others should be the driving force, and thoughts of self should be the last consideration."

Verse 8

Themes:

- Daily Prayer
- Giving Thanks
- Individuality
- Sincerity

"In order to be in tune with God and with your place in the Universal Plan, daily prayer is essential. ~ The very thought of such a commitment may put off some people – but wait! ~ Is your idea of prayer that of kneeling down and repeating certain words from a book? ~ Is it, by saying the right words in the right way, the means of getting what you want? ~ If either of these is true for you, then you are very much off the pathway. ~ Because you were created by God out of Himself*; then there must be a part of God within each one. ~ If your life feels out of tune and feels unloved, then re-establish that link with the Father within and you will find yourself back on your true pathway. ~ No day can truly begin, nor be complete, without that realisation that God is within you and around you always. ~ Saying 'thank you' for the day that is beginning, and asking for the courage and strength to face all that the day may bring, is all that is required. ~ Similarly, at the end of the day, a 'thank you' for the day and all that was experienced, the love of friendship and the beauty that is around you, is the sort of thing that could be expressed. However the prayer is expressed, it should come from the heart and be an expression of joy and thankfulness. ~ If you have experienced great difficulties, then the prayer should still be one of thankfulness for the love and support that helped you through the day. ~ At no time should the prayer be felt as a duty to be got through as quickly as possible. ~ Remember you are speaking to your Beloved, so the prayer should be tender and loving. ~ God is within you and knows exactly

* See Appendix – Note 4.

what you need even before *you* know you need it. ❧ When you speak to your 'earthly beloved' with words of love and appreciation for help given, you would not select a book and read words of love from it. ❧ If you did this, you may be ridiculed or be accused of lacking in sincerity. ❧ Prayer is communication; the linking of one with the Infinite, but just as heartfelt as between lovers. ❧ It is quite usual to feel the need of expressing thankfulness during the day without waiting for the day's end to come. ❧ A pause in your daily activities to allow for a sense of upliftment, while expressing your joy to the Father within, will give the rest of the day a glow it did not have before. ❧ Let it become a habit to give these 'thanks' from the heart as the need arises, and watch your life change for the better."

Verse 9

Themes:
- Lying
- Truth

"How often have you asked yourself: 'What is truth?' ❧ It appears to have a different meaning in different situations. Most of the time 'truth' is relative to the moment. ❧ First of all, each one has to understand what truth really is. ❧ We would say that truth, and all that stems from it, is your understanding of your Father within and your relationship with Him. ❧ When you make a daily communion with your Father then you will know truth, but those who do not have this personal moment with Him, know little of truth. ❧ All will claim to tell the truth, but that is likely to be subjective. ❧ There are others that will bend the whole meaning of truth to suit their own situation. ❧ You were created by the Father and in 'that moment' you knew the truth of your relationship with Him. Now, when there is an instance when truth is needed, you hold that need against your love of the Father and the truth is known. ❧ In doing this, you are living the highest that is within. ❧ If this is always done then you will not stray far from your path of experience. How difficult it is for those who have not communed with the Father in this way, nor have felt the need to do so! Knowing the truth is like having a lamp in the darkness to guide your way. It is not easy to teach truth to those who do not seek the love of the Father, for they do not know the wonder that this relationship brings into one's life. In a material world, the truth of any situation is not understood since the word is glibly used to gain as much profit as is possible. We are not saying that those in commerce are unable to distinguish truth from fiction, but it is easier for them to place spiritual matters in a compartment on its own, to be attended to at a later time. Remember that truth cannot be bought nor bent to suit the waywardness of man, but used in service to others in the highest sense possible. Truth is and cannot be diluted, anything less is not truth."

Verse 10

Themes:

Apartheid · Equality · Racism · Third World · Economic Growth and Power · Unconditional Love

---

"We have said many times that you must love everyone you meet. We accept that it is not possible to like everyone but love them you must. That love must encompass those of other religions and those whose colour of skin is different from your own. The dominance that the white peoples have had over the rest of the world was not intended in the way it has developed. The white peoples had acquired a great amount of knowledge. Knowledge should be shared and not stored away and so it was that the urge to spread this knowledge took hold. These people felt superior and treated those they met in a greedy and cruel way. It was too late to stop this rolling tide of discovery and the dominance of the white peoples began. It has not always worked to their advantage but they did bring new knowledge to others. The World of

Spirit knew that there would come about inequalities, but it was the only way to encourage isolated peoples to step forward. For a great many of your years now, the knowledge that was spread so thinly has been absorbed. ❧ It has been accepted in a different way and is now being turned into an enfolding culture that will become evident as the years pass. ❧ We will warn you now that the way that it will show will be to downgrade the white peoples. ❧ They will receive a teaspoon of their own medicine. ❧ Those who were conquered by force will find that the goods that they make will be forced on the white peoples without choice. ❧ There is much change to come, but as with all change, there will be no sudden movement; it will take hold gradually. ❧ Those who were oppressed by the white peoples will find themselves oppressing them. ❧ We will add here, that the cruelty meted out to the 'so called' ignorant in those far off days, will not be repeated because *they* have grown spiritually. ❧ They have come to understand that the love we urge you all to exercise has become rooted in their races. ❧ All the while there is animosity towards those who are different from yourselves, there will be no real peace."

Verse 11

Themes:

- Day of Judgment
- Fear
- Government Control
- Religious Belief

"Even today many peoples are afraid of God. ❧ It is a fear that has been carried in the races from generation to generation. ❧ It is the result of the so called 'holy men' or 'priests' trying to keep their power over the people. ❧ It is well known that if it is possible to instill fear of something or someone in the masses, then you have control over them. ❧ In time past, most people were ignorant, because few were able to read or write their language and had to rely on what they were told by their religious leaders. ❧ We are surprised to find that such fear still persists because habits die very slowly. We want you to look towards God as your Creator and your benefactor in every way possible. ❧ We want you to be able to go to Him with your troubles and your sorrows. ❧ Speak to Him in the quietness of your inner being without a trace of fear, because God does not favour one above another. ❧ We are all children of the Godhead, and we look towards him for all things needful for our well-being and understanding of His creation. ❧ There is one fear that does still persist; not so much a fear of God, but fear of the Day of Judgment. ❧ Many terrible stories *still* are told today that if certain things are, or are not done, you will be cast into the abyss or Hell on the Day of Judgment! ❧ *You* would not accept such statements from anyone because your eyes have been opened, but there are very many even now, who hold this as a real fear and believe that such a thing could and would happen to them. ❧ It is useless to try and point such souls in a different direction because they have grown with that belief and would be unable to shake it off. We want you to look toward God in love, for God is the very embodiment of Love itself. He is Love and could not cast His children away from Himself for any reason. ❧ If wrong has been done, that soul is helped through Love to put it right. God is Perfect Love and knows nothing of so called Hell or Judgment."

Verse 12

Themes:

- Past Lives
- Soul Memory
- Thoughts

"The knowledge about life eternal – which you may all find an interesting subject – is not just for interest only. ❧ We want you to really understand it and to live it. ❧ Take it piece by piece and absorb it; throwing out that which you know to be rubbish and cherishing that which you know to be true. ❧ We want you to ignore idle curiosity as in: 'Who was I in the last life?' ~ It may be of passing interest to you, but you are not now the same person you were then. ~ Indeed it *could* help some to understand themselves, but there are better ways to do that, more in keeping with the person you have become and are yet to become. ~ While you were in the World of Spirit before this life, you were not just idly passing the time ready for this life. ~ Most of you were preparing yourselves for this life, in order to identify all the experiences that will be necessary for the growth of the Spirit. ~ Although it may seem to you that life is a very haphazard affair and that luck takes a hand, in fact this not so at all. ~ The good things you get are not by luck but by work and understanding. ~ We accept that most of the time you do not have the conscious understanding but right thoughts and kindly actions do bring their reward, though not always immediately. ~ The opposite is true of course. ~ Those who are selfish and hardly ever think of others may wonder what they have to do to have their lives go right. ~ They do sometimes seem to have what you term 'luck' but it does not bring them happiness, because being of a suspicious nature they half expect something unpleasant to happen. ~ We now suggest that whether you were a famous person in the last life or just an ordinary person, leave it all behind. ~ If you were famous then your shortcomings were shown for all to see. ~ We are sure that now you would rather view your failings in private, and leave the 'ego' to those who have further to go in the understanding of the wonders of life that can be lived."

Verse 13

Themes:

- A New Age
- Knowledge
- Other Worlds
- Wisdom

"When you look up and see the night sky and wonder at the myriad points of light that are visible, and you marvel at what you see, at your present state of knowledge, it is still impossible to travel to one of these points of light. We ask, 'Why would you want to reach them?' It has been established by other means, that none of the planets that you see could support human life. In fact, many of those you see and many more that you cannot see do have inhabitants, either as Spiritual beings or in a physical form of life that you know nothing of. If we were to tell about these other Spiritual or physical forms of life, you would not accept what we would say. At the moment it is mere curiosity and that we will not satisfy. The time will come when there will be a different understanding among the peoples of the Earth Plane. Until that time comes it is pointless to discuss matters that are outside your present state of knowledge and understanding. We would urge you to put things right on the Earth Plane first of all, and treat all peoples as your brothers and sisters. In so doing you will learn many things, because your minds will be open and not closed as many are now and the activity will fit you for additional knowledge which Spirit will bring to those who are able to receive. There are many now who are receiving advanced knowledge, but those who hold the reins of power will have nothing to do with it, because they think they know better than channels for Spirit knowledge. There is little you can do at this time but to meditate on it and pray that one day soon those with earthly power will listen, and insist that this knowledge is put before the peoples of the Earth Plane. There will come an Advanced Soul who will realize that after all these centuries of fighting with each other there is another way and will bring it into being. Then will dawn an 'Age of Peace and Understanding' when Spirit will be closer to the Earth Plane than ever before; when *all* peoples will be able to realize happiness while learning within the confines of a physical body and 'fear' will be almost unknown."

Verse 14

Themes:
God Love Evil

"There is only one power or if you prefer energy. That power or energy is termed by you as God or the Great Spirit. This wonderful power is all creative and is absolute Love. The understanding of this Love is outside anything so far encountered by anyone on the Earth Plane. You think you know what pure unconditioned love is, but you do not. It is delicate enough to construct the wings of a butterfly but strong enough to cause the stars and planets to remain in their defined orbits. Every least detail is given such beauty that humans try to copy, but will never succeed because the one important piece would be missing: life. All that grows and moves has that quality that human beings alone cannot give. Only God can bestow life. For that reason alone, God is the Supreme Being. That unconditioned love gives us not only life, but the ability to think and feel, to create beauty and harmony, and also gives us the need to aspire to the highest and best that it is possible to attain. That which you call evil has no power of its own but only the power it is given by the human race. Evil is the turning away from the strength of goodness, from peace and harmony and attempting to destroy that which is beautiful. There are those in the realms of darkness who have turned away from God and wallowed in wickedness. They have enjoyed what they have done and try to influence those on the Earth who are weak. Unfortunately they are often successful, as the activities on the Earth Plane will show. There are many souls who dedicate themselves trying to help these evil beings in darkness. The work is hard and distressing but gradually these hideous beings are shown how they can rise to the light and regain access to God's Love. Never forget that God does not withdraw his Love from even his most disobedient son. The one in darkness has moved out of the light, which is *that* beautiful love that we all bask in and try to understand. ~ Your prayers that light shall penetrate into the minds of those dark beings, will help those who toil to rescue them."

Verse 15

Themes:

- Prayer

"We wish to speak to you about prayer. ~ So often prayers are a few garbled words, hoping that someone out there will hear and bring the desired thing, whatever it may be. ~ We would advise against this practice, because if there is no response and this is usually the case, then disillusion sets in. ~ Of course there will be no answer because that is not prayer. ~ Prayers should be the asking for strength and courage to face the ways of the world. ~ Another prayer is the thinking about one who is suffering or is in need of some healing, and in so doing, setting up the conditions for the Healers in Spirit to administer the healing as is requested in the prayer. ~ These prayers are answered by those in Spirit who wish to help those of Earth. ~ It is no good asking for money or a job or even a new home. These are not things that Spirit are able to supply. ~ It is *you* who must find your way to do those things, as they are the 'things' of Earth. ~ We can help with inspiration and strength to lead towards the realization of the desire. ~ Our advice is to first of all, sit quietly and find that place within where the Spirit of God dwells. ~ If you have not yet found it, then now is the time to set aside a few minutes and be still. ~ Listen for that small voice which cannot be heard above the din of the Earth. ~ Wait in patience, even if it means on several days or even weeks, for we can assure you that patience will be rewarded. ~ You will then know that you have made contact with your God within, for you will find a peace surround you that you have never known before. ~ The wonder of this contact will touch your soul and if there have been prayers before you will know why they were not answered. ~ Do this regularly and you will find that your needs will be met. ~ Here we say 'needs' but by now you will be content, because you will have found something of very great value."

Verse 16

Themes:
Angels Creation Life You

"In the beginning was the Word. ~ That is how your famous book starts but you may ask, 'What was that Word?' ~ We cannot tell you and nor can anyone in your World tell you either. ~ The reason this is so is that we were all a part of that Great Spirit at that time. ~ None of us had become individual beings and therefore were not able to say what happened. We do know it was a very great moment. ~ We do know that creation in visible form started to take place. ~ Although the word 'day' is stated, it was in fact many millions of your Earth years. ~ It was very much later that workers were needed to help to carry out the Plan of Creation. ~ The Supreme Being you name God, could not do the all work that was needed on the Earth Plane because that required Spiritual Beings using a physical body. ~ That was when we were all individualised in order to be the workers. ~ Each one of us has a part to play in this Plan. ~ It may be only a very small part but vital just the same. ~ There is no other who is able to contribute your part however small it may seem to be. ~ Each one is needed and each one is important. ~ You may not think this is true, but because you are where you are, you cannot see the whole picture. ~ We are in a position to see a little further ahead than can you, but we cannot see the whole Plan either. ~ There were others created by the Supreme Being who were to share more particularly than us – the workers. ~ They are known to you as the Angels or the High Guardians of the Plane of the Godhead. ~ Their work is of a very high order, and although they do visit us from time to time, we are not privileged to see them at their work. ~ They are the ones who keep the stars and the planets in their courses, but how they do this we do not know. ~ We can call on them if we have a problem that we cannot find the answer to that we need, or rather the exact explanation that we need. ~ We have found them to be very gentle and kind, but we cannot see them properly because they must heavily veil themselves to visit the lower planes. ~ We understand that in times of real crisis or need they will visit the Earth Plane. ~ Those who receive their help are aware that something wonderful has occurred, and know that the one who suddenly appeared – when needed – was of a special quality. ~ If you have a visit from one of the Shining Ones, that moment will forever remain in your memory."

Verse 17

Themes:

- Conscience
- Incarnation
- Intuition
- Past Lives

"Many have asked why it is necessary to have an Earth incarnation when any necessary instruction could be given while in the Spirit Realms without the need for an Earth life. If deeper thought was given to this idea it would be realized that there is nothing like experience for the teaching it brings, to be firmly etched in one's being. ~ It is quite possible to learn things from a teacher or from a book, but when it comes to personal wisdom then the only means of true learning is to experience with one's whole being. ~ If the learning comes from making a mistake, then after the experience, there is a promise to the self never to go through that again. ~ That feeling could not be obtained from a book for all that happened stays as a reminder. ~ We do accept that there are souls who do make the same mistakes over again and do not learn from them. ∾ They will require much help and guidance from Spirit. ∾ There are those who wish that the experience from previous lives on the Earth Plane could be brought forward into this life memory, but that could have unfortunate consequences. ∾ It would not be possible to have only some of the previous experiences but to ignore others. ∾ Your past life experience may have come from a position of power and privilege, but to bring that into a present life, which may be one of many difficulties and perhaps even poverty, would cause even more unhappiness, as constant comparisons would be made. ∾ The wisdom of the Father of Love gives each one a veil over the memory from a previous life. ∾ However, you do carry with you a conscience, which is the essence of all previous experiences and will make itself known. ∾ It will stand in front of all actions and will tell you if a certain course is unwise; *then* it is wise to take notice. ∾ If you override your conscience and frequently do so, it will become muffled and will no longer be your guiding star. ∾ Listen to that voice of conscience; it is the wisdom of many lives."

Verse 18

Themes:

Self-Love · The Body (alcoholism, anorexia, bulimia, low self esteem, overweight, self loathing, substance abuse)

"In order to live a life on Earth that is both successful and productive it is necessary to love yourself. ∾ On the face of it, it may seem arrogant and selfish, but if you examine it closely you will find this is not so. ∾ If you are caring for those in your family that you love, you will do your very best for them, so that they are happy and comfortable. ∾ If there is conflict or misunderstanding, you would want to do all you could to help them to enjoy life again. ∾ If you would feel that way about those you love, why not feel the same way about yourself? You are equally important to those you wish to help. ᔓ If you love yourself, you are saying thank you to the Great Spirit for the life you have been given and the body in which to live, while trying to bring love and happiness to others. ᔓ If you love yourself, you will take care of that same body and look after it, as you would look after those you love. ᔓ Remember, that a well cared for healthy body is better able to help others and be of service to all who need it. ᔓ We are not speaking about extremes of self-love, such as vanity and posing before others. ᔓ We only wish to convey that care and concern for the self is as necessary as listening to the wise counsel that is available from your helpers in Spirit. ᔓ Those who decry the body as being something to put up with – in fact – almost a vile thing are doing themselves a grave disservice. ᔓ More often as not, care for that body will be minimal and the sustenance will often be of poor quality. ᔓ The reason for this is found in the belief that more good works can be done if the self is ignored. ᔓ This attitude will easily lead to an attack of depression, which will get deeper as hatred of the body grows. If such souls can be taught to love themselves and realize self worth, the depression will lift and a happier life will be the result. ᔓ In all lives there are difficult periods to work through, but this should not stop a sensible degree of self-love. Ask for daily blessings from the Great Spirit that your joy in service will be full."

Verse 19

Themes:
Balance · Body · Overwork · Stress

"Your earthly body is your most precious possession; without it you could not live upon the Earth Plane and therefore, it should be afforded all the care and consideration that you can give. ᔓ It will do your bidding to the extremes of endurance, provided you will give it sufficient rest. ~ Your body is very finely balanced. ~ It works best within a narrow range of temperature and outside of it will indicate that it is sick and needs urgent attention. ~ Your body continually informs you when it needs food, liquid and rest and will tell you whether it is too hot or too cold. ~ What a wonderful piece of engineering! ~ We wonder how many of you realize this and stop and think of it? ~ So often mistreated, it only complains when it has put up with too much. ~ The wrong food or too much strong drink will quickly make these things known, but there are other factors which take time to react upon the body sufficiently to insist that its owner takes notice. ~ We know that the type of life that each of you is called upon to accept, is not always good for your wonderful body. ~ Often you work longer than the body should endure without enough rest, and here we mean mental rest as well as body rest. ~ You are much more than your body; you are a Spiritual Being and too much pressure and demands upon your body, without a thought for your mental and spiritual well-being, is bringing you to imbalance. ~ Some call this stress, but it is imbalance between the material, mental and spiritual bodies. ~ We urge you to think about this before it brings to you the pain and struggle with this imbalance. ~ Give yourself a few moments of mental rest during your busy days. ~ Each morning before you start your day's activity ask God to give you strength and guidance for the day ahead; then your body will enjoy balance, to enable it to give of its best."

Verse 20

Themes:
- Higher Self
- Incarnation
- Intuition
- Soul Purpose
- Spiritual Laws

"Many question the need to come back to a life on the Earth Plane. ~ You are not compelled to come back against your will. ~ The only reason for a return to the Earth is to experience and learn the lessons so necessary for the progress that we all speak of and encourage. ~ If you were compelled to return you would be no more than puppets. ~ We want you to remember that the entire course of progress from the moment you were individualised to the far reaches of eternity is made under the Law of Love alone. ~ Because the Law of Love is always in operation, you must follow your own Spirit and take your own time to understand and accept the laws that govern all things Spiritual. ~ There is no race to determine who can get there first. ~ There are many who willingly slow down in order to help the less able to catch up, and without realising it speed up their own progress. ~ It is the Law of Love – which is above all other laws – that allows each one the freedom to progress as they feel able. ~ It is quite possible to make some progress while remaining in the World of Spirit but sooner or later there is an inner-longing for more understanding. ~ All your knowledge and experience as a Spiritual Being is stored in your 'higher self' which can only be accessed in the stillness. ~ It is only when you set aside the material world and go into the silence that you reach the guidance for the next step. ~ Those who do not, often find themselves in trouble, because they cannot find the help they need from a material world. Many just *know* the right way for them and they call it intuition, which is the total of your experience bringing you the best way. ~ Those who find the Earth life bewildering are usually new souls who do not have enough experience to draw upon; they need a helping hand. ~ At every step on the way, realise that the love you embrace and follow, is the ever flowing love of your Creator."

Verse 21

Themes:
- Healing
- Helping Others

"Many of you are aware of the value of healing and many have received it from a healer at some time. ∾ As you know, healing is not always the laying-on of hands. ∾ Those who offer a word of encouragement, or of support for those who are weighed down by life's problems, do a great deal of good work. When you feel really down, there is comfort in knowing that another understands and has come to give words to lift the soul. ∾ That too is healing; it is the expression of love – one to another – in the true way of brothers and sisters. ∾ Any words and thoughts of comfort you can give to others when there is need, is a form of healing. ∾ You may ask what healing really is? ∾ We have often heard the question asked. People of Earth must always know what things are about and the power of healing is no exception. ∾ Deep within your own being you know the answer, for it is the Love directly from the Creator of All that is channelled through the healer to ease the suffering of the one to be healed. ∾ All people can act as healers in a greater or lesser capacity. ∾ If you offer love to another you offer a form of healing. ∾ Those who are designated healers are those who are especially suitable to carry their Creator's Love from His helpers, to the soul in need of it. ∾ It comes through many channels to reach the Earth Plane but the cleaner the channel, the stronger the power of that wondrous Love. ∾ If you are sincere in your desire to help another who is in need, then in whatever way you feel able to help, those in Spirit will come to your assistance and bring that which is needed. ∾ Never doubt that Spirit is ever waiting to help those who try to ease the burden of others. ∾ Do not fear that you will deplete yourself by giving so freely of help and healing, there is always some over to maintain the giver in good health to continue the work."

Verse 22

Themes:
- Autumn & Winter
- Habits
- Meditation
- Prejudices
- Reflection

"This is a time of much activity; the trees shed their leaves and draw down their life force during the cold of winter. ~ It is a time when gardeners prune their trees and bushes to discard all that is dead and of no further use. ~ It is also a good time for each one to turn within and take stock of one's own growth or lack of it, during these many months. ~ It is a timely reminder when you see the leaves falling that much unnecessary personal baggage can also be shed. ~ All the old ideas and prejudices can be cast aside if each one is taken out and examined. ~ In most cases it will be found that these are burdens that should have been cast out long ago. ~ Now is the time to heal any area of personal conflict and misunderstanding. ~ Getting rid of burdens that have weighed you down is not easy, for they have become a habit, but the pruning has to be harsh sometimes to bear better fruit eventually. ~ This is a time when going into the silence can be of the greatest benefit. ~ It is when the clamour of everyday life is shut out for a short while and the sensitive and even painful areas can be brought to the surface of the mind. ~ It is then that you are closer to Spirit, and if their help is asked for, then much can be resolved and healed. ~ Time spent in this way is not wasted, but can bring upliftment and healing in the knowledge that when your burdens are placed in the light of Spirit, a way to overcome the difficulties can be seen more easily. ~ It is often easier to help another and see a way through *their* problems, than see the way through your own. ~ Perhaps that is the way to solve some problems. ~ Find a reliable confidante and mirror your problems by discussing them. ~ Personal pruning of failed ideas and negative thinking will lighten your journey through life, and by asking for God's blessing – everyday – on *all* your endeavours to lead you onward in peace and harmony."

Verse 23

Themes:
Hate · Unconditional Love · War

"So often, we urge those of the Earth Plane to love everyone that they meet without question, and without condition. ೲ You do not have to like all those you meet, but love them you must. ೲ This may seem difficult to some, but when thought is given to the matter it is easily understood. ೲ God created you out of Himself and out of Love. ೲ When you are called upon to help one in trouble, you do not ask which God he worships nor do you note the colour of his skin; that is giving love without condition. ೲ It saddens us very greatly to see so much hatred still present on the Earth Plane. ೲ Much of the hatred is handed down the generations and has become a habit. ೲ Many with such hate worship their Creator with real sincerity and yet cannot bring together the love for their God to include love for their fellows. ೲ Even the very young are taught to hate, almost before they can speak their own language. ೲ You have means of communication now that should be helping the peoples of the world to understand each other, and to begin to remove the old ways which led to misunderstanding and therefore mistrust. ೲ It is now possible to bring diverse peoples together to discuss their differences, and arrive at a solution of their problems, and yet hatred still persists. ೲ Send thoughts of love to all who hate. ೲ Those of you who do this will begin to make a difference. ೲ We are trying from the World of Spirit, to impress the mind that is filled with hatred, to turn and look at his neighbour in a different light and learn to extend the hand of friendship. There are a few who are beginning to hear the whisper of Spirit from within and act upon it, but it is a slow process so we ask you to join with us in sending loving thoughts to the troubled areas. ೲ In this way we can all help to do the Will of God, to spread His Love throughout the Earth Plane. ೲ Give out love every day and you will receive love in abundance."

Verse 24

Themes:
Ignorance · Judgement · Prejudice

"It appears to us that most people of the Earth Plane are prejudiced in one way or another. ~ Some maintain that 'theirs' is an open mind, while secretly harbouring a prejudice; but others do admit to some prejudices. ~ We do ask ourselves why this should be? ~ The very word means that the subject under consideration has been prejudged; that a decision has been reached about it, without first seeing it or contacting it in some way. ~ How can this be? ~ If someone offers any of you a food or a drink that you have not tasted, how can you decide that you do not like it before trying even the smallest amount? ~ Likewise, the prejudice which abounds against the colour of another's skin; how can you judge without first meeting the person in question? ~ In many cases it is not even judging by appearances. ~ Judgement is often made in advance without any contact or description whatever. ~ That can never be the best way of going about one's life; where everything is prejudged without any personal assessment. ~ In this way the life becomes bounded by so many rules, made up as the journey proceeds, that it is entirely hidebound* with no give and take whatever. ~ This is when superstition takes over and more rules are devised to counteract the 'bad luck' – so called – that comes about by the first set of personal rules. How complicated life becomes under these circumstances. ~ We would advise that anyone caught up in any hint of the words we have already given, to now cut loose and be yourself. ~ If you must make any judgement, make it with the eye of understanding and experience, and do not fall into the trap of judging before you know for real the situation that presents itself. ~ Not one of you would like to be prejudged – usually unfavourably – before contact is made. ~ So many other things come under this heading that it needs some quiet

* Hidebound – restricted by petty rules and unwilling to accept new ideas.

contemplation to root it out before it takes hold. ❧ Ask the Father of all Wisdom to give you the insight to judge wisely and compassionately and learn to love everyone."

Verse 25

Themes:
Fear · Materialism · Stress · Unhappiness

"When we draw close to the Plane of Earth we can feel the unrest that engulfs it. ❧ Formerly it was one of the ills of the poorer peoples, but now it can be seen among those who appear to have all that your world can offer, and yet *they* are not at peace. ❧ We do not mean that they will take to the streets and loudly shout their displeasure but it shows itself in other ways. ❧ There is more mental strain than ever there was in former days. ❧ So much effort has to be put into earning a living to supply the needs of the family, that those who work thus have little or no time for the children of the family, so instead of drawing together they drift apart. ❧ Those under this strain visit a doctor to obtain help, but there is no help except drugs to calm the unrest of the mind. ❧ The Great Spirit did not intend that the human body should be filled with drugs in order to maintain some semblance of living. ❧ The 'god' that is worshiped is no longer the Father of all Creation but instead: the god of material gain. ❧ That 'god' has largely taken over to the detriment of the human race and unrest has been the result. ❧ There will be no improvement until those addicted to gathering more wealth come to see that in the end, they have nothing that has substance. ❧ For all the effort, nothing of that wealth can be taken with you when it is time to pass into the World of Spirit. ❧ Even while on the Earth that wealth is not truly enjoyed, so why strain so much to get it? ❧ How naked you would find yourself in Spirit! ❧ We would ask you to fulfil your commitment of work, but use any spare time to bring peace, joy and security to your family by your presence. ❧ We hope that you will remember your Father in your quiet moments, and ask Him for courage and strength to face each new day without strain. ❧ Ask Him too, for His Love and Blessings to flood the world."

Verse 26

Themes:
- Helpers & Guides
- Life in Spirit

"We often speak of progress, and we know that many of you would like to know about progress in the World of Spirit. ❧ We want to assure you that there is very little difference. Progress is made through the giving of service to others and, as on the Plane of Earth, service can take many forms. Sometimes, just listening to the troubles of another will help them to see a way through their problems. ❧ Service is the setting aside of 'self' to give comfort to another on the path of life. ❧ In the World of Spirit the giving of service does not change. ❧ There are countless beings that are willing to set aside their own progress – for a period – in order to inspire and advise those of the Earth Plane, and are known as Guides and Helpers. ❧ They have specific knowledge that could be of benefit to their chosen charge. ❧ It is their way of giving service and also making some progress for themselves. ❧ All help given to those of Earth benefits the Helper, because the Helper learns much in the course of the Earth contact and a great love develops between them. ❧ Then comes the time to move on, for often, without realising it, the Helper has given much and has moved into a new area of expression; there is a new understanding which has come from the Earth contact. ❧ It is as though the landscape has changed and a new path has shown itself with new challenges for service. ❧ All around and about there is less to remind the aspirant* of the Earth Plane and everything has a finer more lustrous quality. ❧ It has

* Aspirant: a person or Spirit Guide who wants to do better things.

come about so gradually that at first the awareness was vague, but now it has become more obvious and a greater sensitivity pervades one's being. ~ There is a new sense of longing to be of more service, and as if by a magnetic pull, one is led towards a group of like-minded souls who will show the next step on the pathway of progress. ~ Gradually the drawing power of Earth will diminish, and even greater joy will be found in the service that can be undertaken – which is quite unlike that which has gone before."

Verse 27

Themes:
Ego (I) Greater Self (We)

"You may have asked yourselves why it is that we do not use the 'I' instead of the 'We' that is customary? ~ If the 'I' is used it stresses the individual – the ego. ~ In the World of Spirit there is no longer an 'I'. ~ All thought and effort is the result of a collective effort. ~ We draw *all* our words of wisdom from the well of truth that comes through the spheres of being from the Higher Realms of Light and Radiance. ~ That which is filtered down for us to use, starts out as a serene and blissful picture. ~ That picture gradually unfolds itself to us and the words are formulated for the benefit of those of Earth who wish to hear and read. ~ We interpret the picture we see before us, after we have tuned our beings to understand that which is being sent. ~ We could not therefore use the 'I' because in those circumstances the 'I' no longer exists. ~ You are able to use the 'I' because you are a facet of the whole you, and normally you are not able to consult with and receive from the whole you. ~ The facet then becomes the 'I' because it has to choose for itself – for right or wrong – and is responsible for its action. ~ There are those who are aware of the 'greater self' and are able to draw wisdom from it, but the 'you' on Earth – the facet – is still responsible for the life now being undertaken.

Those who are able to draw wisdom from Spirit will find life much more rewarding, but Spirit will not attempt to live your life for you. ~ You still have lessons to learn and difficulties to overcome even with the wisdom of Spirit. ~ While the harder lessons are being learnt, you will know that you have the strength and support of Spirit at all times. ~ Even at the blackest moment there will be peace in your inner-being, and you will know that with God's blessing, you will triumph. When you return to Spirit you will better understand that you have *always* been part of the whole."

Verse 28

Themes:

- Contentment
- Faith
- Inner Peace
- The Supreme Being
- Tranquillity

"Just as a ship needs a safe anchorage from the storms that beset it, so do we need a safe anchorage. ~ We need a place of safety and a lifeline when the 'storms of life' rage around us. Each of us has that lifeline and hopefully that place of safety, if it could only be recognised as such. ~ The lifeline may be one's belief in a Being or Power greater than the self. ~ You may not be able to give that Being a name, but awareness of it is all that is required in times of stress. ~ Ideally, each one should be aware of this Supreme Being at all times, but in the crush of everyday life such things are often forgotten. ~ The place of safety is within one's own being. ~ When the storms are raging all around and you do not know which way to turn, then going 'within' is to find that safe anchorage. ~ There you will find the peace that will give rest to your weary soul and the voice of Love to soothe your aching heart. ~ Those who do not bother with such things will find great difficulty in claiming this anchorage, but with daily practice it will be an automatic reaction when the going gets tough. ~ Each visit will bring strength to you and you will always feel able to face anything life can throw in your direction. ~ During each day cultivate your awareness of the Supreme Being. ~ To do this, be aware of Nature in all its glory and loveliness, and with this awareness well to the fore, it will lead you to your place of safety in times of stress and commotion. ~ By using all of this, you will maintain a centre of peace and tranquillity and the world will not be able to disturb your safety. ~ This does not mean that the lessons that *need* to be learned will be bypassed, far from it! ~ But from within, can be drawn the courage and blessings to go forward. ~ You will be led by Spirit and no harm will come to you even in the darkest hour. ~ Place your faith in that which is greater than you and you cannot fail."

Verse 29

Themes:
- Greater Self
- Reincarnation
- The Journey of the Soul

"Many questions are asked about reincarnation and many different answers are given. ~ We say there is reincarnation but we can understand the apparent confusion. ~ Let us explain it like this: on previous occasions we have likened an Earth visit to the polishing of the facet of a diamond. ~ The whole you does *not* incarnate; only the part of you that needs the particular experience that an incarnation – at this time – will offer. ~ The experience *must* coincide with the conditions that will prevail, in order to obtain that experience. ~ It may seem to some as 'potluck' as to whether the life being lived is meaningful or not. ~ Incarnation is not an accident as it would sometimes appear. ~ When the Wise Ones have advised that circumstances *will* offer the conditions for a particular experience, then you would be shown the parents and the life framework that *you* would experience. ~ Although you would be urged to follow the advice of the Wise Ones, you still have the gift of free will and could, even at that point, refuse to accept. ꟹ If you agree to take the advice and the good counselling that would be given, then the process towards the incarnation is begun. ꟹ Throughout the life on Earth, the 'greater-self' will closely follow the experiences that are undertaken. ꟹ On occasions it has been known for the greater-self to step in, in almost dramatic fashion, to steer their protégé away from imminent danger. ꟹ This greater-self will help protect and guard that earthly facet from any harm that would prevent the experience from taking place. ꟹ When that small part of the whole returns to the World of Spirit and is reunited with the whole, the lessons learned will enhance the whole rather like the polishing of the facet of the diamond. ꟹ At a later stage, which could be hundreds of years in Earth time, it may be necessary for another part of the whole to undergo experiences that would advance the whole in further spiritual progress. ꟹ Since the whole benefits from the experience of each facet, *that* – to us – answers the question of reincarnation. ꟹ The processes and understanding involved are more complicated than we have stated, but they will serve to offer an explanation."

Verse 30

Themes:
- The Supreme Being

"All that is, was created by God or whatever name you give to the Supreme Being. ꟹ That statement has been made by countless people and in many different words, but *still* humankind does not really accept the meaning behind the words. ꟹ Again we tell you that God is not an old man somewhere in the sky. ꟹ No one can see God in the visual sense of the word. ꟹ God is an infinite creative energy that is the very essence of Love itself. ꟹ All that was and is created, is through Love itself, and for that reason God is all around you, in all you touch, see, and in the very food you eat.

Therefore those who are earnestly seeking God must be aware that, *'In Him we live and move and have our being.'* ৺ This is a statement that was made a long time ago and is still relevant. Be aware of the God that is, in this visual sense. ৺ To find the God you seek you must go 'within,' into the silence, and there is the Divine Spark; not in the roar of the material life but by being still. ৺ That does not only mean by *keeping* still, but to *still* the mind so that the small voice – that is the Divine – can be heard. ৺ Have patience, for one day you will succeed. ৺ Hold it close to your heart, for it will sustain you in difficult moments and be as a refuge when you feel you cannot go on. ৺ As we have said before, speak lovingly to the God within, for He is part of you and you are part of Him. ৺ These precious moments should not be spoken about, but you can guide others to the understanding and realisation of this illumination of the soul. ৺ Once you find this precious jewel within, your life will be transformed because, what you once believed you now know. ৺ Most who embark on this course try too hard and quickly become disillusioned when the goal seems as far away as ever. ৺ Feel a sense of humility and have patience, for in a moment when you least expect, you will know your Beloved is there and ecstasy will infuse your being."

Verse 31

Themes:
Life's Lessons The Souls Journey

"The Earth Plane acts as a melting pot for all sorts and types of people. ৺ This mixture is composed of those who are spiritually advanced as well as those who are largely ignorant. The fact that there is such a mixture, offers the background for the ability to learn the valuable lessons that each one is sent to learn. ৺ Many have said that when the time comes for the transition to Spirit they will not return to the Earth Plane – no matter what advice is given – because of the unpleasant experiences that have been endured. ෴ You would find it very difficult to learn the necessary lessons in Spirit, and before long you would feel the pull of the Earth Plane to do the learning. There is one point that should be borne in mind if such thoughts do come into your thinking; in the course of the learning of lessons while in a physical body, you are able to influence and help others while you are learning; almost like paying your way. ෴ Many a lesson is learned in the process of helping another through a difficult patch, or giving the benefit of previous experience to overcome a particular problem. ෴ Much knowledge can be absorbed from the pages of a book, but to make that knowledge your own, and firmly entrenched in your being, is to experience it. ෴ Hands on knowledge will make its mark and will always be remembered. ෴ In the World of Spirit the rule is: like attracts like. ෴ When you pass to this side of life you will find you are with people just like yourself so that learning from among them would be limited. ෴ You could visit a lower plane, but still you would find it difficult to experience the valuable lessons that Earth could offer. ෴ In the course of time, you would become so frustrated that you would willingly take up another life on the Earth Plane. ෴ Remember that the Great Spirit knows the ways of men and women, and knows that the 'feeling of frustration' – or something akin to it – will put that soul back on the path of progress as was previously planned."

Verse 32

Themes:
- Manifestation
- The Power of Thought
- Universal Truth

"Many times you have been told that the moment after 'so called' death, you are still the same person and have not suddenly become an angel! ෴ While on the Earth Plane you have become accustomed to using your mind and your brain.

~ The ideas that form in the mind are then translated by the brain into activities that the physical body can undertake. ~ In the World of Spirit you no longer have a brain as such, and each thought is brought into being immediately. ~ At first this is a novelty, but you soon become accustomed to it. ~ It is then that you realise that thoughts are things. ~ This is something that we have tried to impress on the Earth minds but with little avail. ~ As soon as you start to formulate your thoughts, they are taking shape in the ether that is all around you. ~ The more you think that thought, the stronger it gets and will soon come into being. ~ There is an overall tendency to think the worst about any given situation. ~ The worst possible outcome is gone over again and again, and when it does, there is a cry as to why this terrible thing should happen? ~ Now you can see why: your thinking has created it. ~ If you think in a positive way about a possible outcome, you will not be surprised at a happy result. ~ Give it a try and prove that thoughts are things and you can create good, happy situations instead of the worst. ~ Be warned – do not slip back into the old negative ways. ~ If you do, all your effort is cancelled and you will have to start again. ~ As with most things it a matter of practice but you must watch your thoughts. ~ Outline a positive way of life for yourself now, and make all your thinking happy and positive. ~ When things do not turn out the way you had hoped, we hope that you will go over your thinking before the result became known, and then *know* where you let yourself down. ~ Gradually you will understand the truth of our message to you."

Verse 33

Themes:

- Prayer

"We have touched on prayer before in our words to you, but it does seem to be stumbling block for many people. ~ For prayer to be effective, the position of the body is of no importance. ~ If, however, a certain position makes you feel ready for prayer then do it, but it is not necessary. ~ The important part is your thinking. ~ It is what you are thinking that brings the prayer to action. ~ A set form of words is not to be recommended either, because after a while those words become a sort of habit to be got through. ~ Real prayer comes from the heart – words full of feeling and compassion. ~ For instance, when a loved one is sick you would pray from the heart with all your feeling put into it. ~ That is the kind of prayer that will bring the help you need. ~ That feeling can be broadened to encompass those you do not know but their need is just as great – whatever that need is. ~ It may be food, shelter or freedom from being attacked. ~ Whoever they are and wherever they are, they are like your loved ones when in need. ~ We do not recommend that you should pray for more of what you have already; that is a waste of effort and will not have the desired result. ~ Your prayers would be more fruitful if you asked for more wisdom to help you live your life more fully. ~ Ask for strength and courage in order to face the future in a positive way. ~ There is a form of prayer that is often overlooked: whenever you see something of beauty say a 'thank you' for the privilege of being able to witness it. ~ At your mealtimes say a silent 'thank you' for the food you are about to eat; being aware that there are so many who will not be able to do that. ~ If you make a practice of these suggestions you will find you are becoming more balanced, because of less emphasis on the ego. ~ Allow the wonder of nature and compassion for others to play a larger part in your spiritual enfoldment, and you will become aware of many blessings."

Verse 34

Themes:
Charity · Giving · Laws of Spirit · Truth of Spirit

"Each time we are able to communicate with you we wish to emphasise the Truths of Spirit. ❧ We have tried to show you that your heavenly Father – or that which you call God – is in all things. ❧ Without that pure love energy, nothing would exist in your world or in any of the many other worlds. ❧ Spirit cannot be divided into little packages, and for that reason there is a spark of God within each one, however well it appears to be hidden. ❧ You cannot be separated from God even if you do not believe in that wondrous Being. ❧ It is for that reason that we must look upon each other as our brothers and sisters, because we cannot separate ourselves from that divinity. ❧ Those who have little of the world's goods cannot help those less fortunate even than themselves, but they can send out their thoughts of healing and loving kindness each day to them. ❧ It is an attitude of mind that is of great importance. ❧ Even the giving of money or goods to help the needs of others do little for the giver if the attitude of mind is wrong. ❧ When you give to another or to a good cause, it is wise to bless the goods or the money that is being given. ❧ Send it out with your love to the one who will receive, and in the course of time, you yourself will receive a blessing that *you* may need at that time. ❧ To give, because it looks the right thing to do, does *not* have this effect because the giving has gone out with a negative attitude. ❧ Nor must you do it in order to gain from it; that will attract the wrong reaction to you. ❧ The right attitude is one of a desire to help another and the blessing to go with it, even if you cannot give materially. ❧ There will come a time when the Truths and Laws of Spirit will be understood and accepted throughout your world. ❧ We know that this may be a long time away but all enlightened peoples are already working towards it. ~ It is for this reason that we, on our side of life, are willing to set our progress aside in order to help those on the Earth Plane to learn and accept those Laws which are for the benefit of all peoples, whether incarnate or discarnate. ~ Eventually all God's creation will beat with the same heart and accept the Law of Spirit without question."

Verse 35

Themes:

- The Earth Plane is an Illusion

"The Earth Plane is a world of illusion. ~ Immediately, you will say that it is solid and therefore it is *not* an illusion. ~ Now we want you to think carefully. ~ It has been proven that no two people see the same thing in the same way. ~ Ask several people to describe an event that has just taken place and you will find as many different answers as the number of people questioned. ~ It is because each one will interpret what they see from *their* own point of view, which is coloured by their life experience and even perhaps by their upbringing and education. ~ There are other instances like those who have suddenly fallen in love with each other, and from then on their world is indeed rose-tinted! ~ Both those examples show that the world is an illusion. ~ It could be that you see what you want to see, or it could be that the scene in front is coloured by your state of mind. ~ If you have to wait a long time in a cold draughty place for a bus or a train, the time spent in waiting will seem to go on much longer than the actual time that has passed. ~ Similarly, when you are with people whose company you enjoy, the time will appear to pass very quickly. ~ It is the same with holidays; the time seems to pass all too quickly before it is time to return home. ~ This apparent illusion experience is a good thing because it can teach much. ~ When things appear to go wrong in life you start to worry and the world looks a very bleak place. ~ Here, it is *your* state of mind that has changed and not the scene that is around you. Once you get to grips with your problem and find a solution to it, your world seems normal again; once the worry of the problem is lifted. ~ In this way Spirit can teach many lessons to those whose minds are open and prepared to learn. ~ The illusion of the Earth Plane can be used to great advantage. Your five senses are your windows on the world but they do not tell you all that you would like to know. ~ You do have an extra sense or a sixth sense* which can be brought into play, but we want you to realise that it is wise to acknowledge the illusory nature of the Earth Plane before adding to the confusion."

Verse 36

Themes:

- Advanced Spiritual Knowledge
- Aura
- Choice
- Energy Field

"There are many threads that form the 'reins of life' for each one. ~ As you progress through the experience of the life you have been given, you pull on one or more of the threads according to the needs of the moment. ~ Perhaps there is provocation when there may be the 'instant need' to pull on the 'thread of anger.' ~ Then, unless cancelled quickly, the pull may be so hard that the next few moments will be regretted later. ~ There are other times when you see or hear of a situation where the 'thread of love' has been the only guiding factor in a life full of difficulties and misunderstandings. Whichever thread you pull on – in the heat of the moment – will either rebuke you or bring you a blessing. ~ Some of these threads are golden, and together with the others will

* Sixth sense: feeling – refer to Verse 45.

present a pattern which can be very beautiful. ~ Its beauty will depend on which threads have been used most often to guide that life forward. ~ In a moment of despair, you may grab the 'thread of self-pity' which has *no* movement, and if indulged in for long will bring life to a standstill; the pattern that unfolds will be shown as a truly grey area. ~ Ask for help if this happens. ~ All these threads are of different colours depending on the quality that it brings. ~ Love brings a beautiful rose pink, which enfolds as well as calms the Spirit, but if that love is tainted by the need to control or demand a return, then its shade becomes a muddy, unpleasant colour. ~ It is the negative reaction to a situation that makes the colour unpleasant and will change the course of the journey when *that* particular thread is grasped. ~ You may not have created the situation, but it is the reaction to it that holds the key to which threads you pull on in a moment of stress. ~ Think before you grab your threads, because it could so easily cause your life to feel insecure and unstable. ~ Ask your Father to guide you every day and take hold of the most beautiful threads to lead your life. ~ It is the daily choices that make the interweaving of the threads a thing of beauty."

Verse 37

Themes:

- Understanding the Truth of Reincarnation

"The question that is often asked is that of reincarnation. ~ We have spoken of it before but now we take it up again. ~ There are many from your side of life who say that reincarnation is not possible and firmly believe so. ~ We say that reincarnation is a fact, but first we must examine what is meant by reincarnation. ~ Those who say it is not possible mean that the *same* personality is not sent back again. ~ To understand this rather more fully, we always insist that only a small part of the whole is ever incarnating at one time. ~ As we have explained at a previous time we liken it to a facet of a diamond; that *very small part* needs to undergo certain experiences in order to be raised to a higher level; rather like the polishing of the facet of the diamond. ~ When that particular set of experiences is fully understood, there will be no further need for that part to incarnate again. ~ That small part does not represent 'the whole' which *never* incarnates in its entirety. ~ The 'greater self' is the Guardian Angel and conscience of the incarnating facet. ~ At some future time, another facet will incarnate to experience and grow in wisdom to raise that to a higher level, and so forth. ~ That is why many say that there is no reincarnation, because that same facet or personality does not keep being sent back to the Earth Plane. ~ In actual fact it may, under some conditions, need to send that *same* facet back again because there was no progress at all during the life just completed. ~ Some say that under conditions of war when lives are cut short, that they will incarnate again but we still think our understanding is the correct one. ~ We say that because we are *all* at different stages of comprehension. ~ What you are able to understand and accept now will be open to change as you progress through the many layers of advanced thought and experience. ~ For this reason alone, we again urge you to meditate every day, in order to touch the deeper truths that are available to ponder over and enrich your own spiritual experience."

Verse 38

Themes:
Anxiety · Depression · Desperation · Fear · Life Purpose* · Loneliness · Meditation · Suicide

---

"As we draw close to your world we can feel the sadness felt by many. ~ There is a feeling of desperation that whatever effort is made the achievement is short lived. ~ Those who have

* Life Purpose: see Appendix – Note 1.

these 'very real' feelings have looked to the future and hoped for brightness but cannot see any. ∾ We say these feelings stem from a sense of being alone, that no-one seems to care. ∾ You are never alone; there is *always* someone with you who loves you deeply. ∾ This, we know, does not always bring the comfort that we hope it would, but much of the feeling of isolation is because you have forgotten that you were created out of the substance of the Godhead. ∾ At the moment you were individualised you were needed to be part of the Plan of Creation. ∾ Your many visits to Earth were intended that you should learn *all* that will be needed to actively take your place within it. ∾ The feelings of isolation are because your origin has been forgotten. ∾ Your Mother and Father created your coat of flesh for your Earth visit, and because of it you honour them as your parents, but you forget the Creator of your individual Spirit. ∾ We want you to daily remember your Father God as you would remember your earthly Father and Mother. ∾ Be aware you are not separate, but *forever* a part of the Godhead. ∾ It is for this reason that we urge you to set aside a few moments of your busy life to speak with your Father within. ∾ Tell Him of your hopes and fears and ask Him to help you to understand the purpose of your life at this time. ∾ If you do this you will receive many of the answers you are seeking. ∾ **There *is* a purpose to your life.** ∾ All that God has created is a part of Himself, and you are just as important as His Angels who are ever with Him. ∾ Feel the beauty that is all around and know that you are a part of that beauty. When you think you are alone, that is the time to go within and speak with your Father who will give you that feeling of inner peace."

Verse 39

Themes:
Peace · Religious Disharmony · War

"Peace is always at the top of the list when prayers are offered for all on the Earth Plane. ~ Those of the world want everyone to live in peace and prosperity but there is little sign of it. ~ It seems that as soon as peace is achieved in one area then there is an uprising in another place. ~ Sometimes the cause is cruelty and hardship inflicted on the people by one man; many of the troubles we see are through religion. Throughout the history of the Earth Plane war has been the result where there have been differences over the practices in religion. ~ Religion should be the means of approaching the Supreme Being or God if you prefer. ~ Most people need some guidance in the method which an individual feels appropriate. ~ All religions have a holy book to which they can refer, or if those people are unable to read, there is one who can explain *their* particular creed to their followers. ~ One would imagine that such a system would be peaceful, but unfortunately there is always *one* who wishes to dominate others and force some other belief on the populace. ~ It is *then* that there bodes trouble for the future if this domination persists. ~ We know that in the past religion has been used to control the people through fear, but this in itself did not lead to open warfare in the name of religion. ~ Those who recognise that the Supreme Being created all that is, and therefore should be worshiped and glorified, know that it is everyone's right to be able to do this in their own way and without interference. ~ Neither the name nor the means by which this is done should be the cause of conflict, one with another. ~ We want all to be able to worship *their* God in the name of Love. ~ All paths lead to the Godhead but the choice of path must be left to the individual. ~ It is this peace of choice that we all pray for, that will capture the hearts and minds of all who accept the

Supreme Being as Creator of all that is. ~ Ask a blessing of peace on all who would fight their fellows and instead offer glory to their God."

Verse 40

Themes:
- Living in the NOW
- Stress
- Worry
- Your Life Plan

"So much stress and strain is caused to human kind by worry. We have seen that the worry is not always because of events around their community. ~ Most of the worry seems to stem from who they are or, who they think they ought to be! ~ Many females wish that their faces were different or their hair was a different colour; and the men are concerned about becoming bald, or that they are too fat or too thin. ~ We say why be so worried about such matters which are purely physical and have no bearing on the 'real' you. ~ The reason that you agreed to incarnation at this time was to experience more of the lessons that the Earth Plane could offer, and that *your* spirituality would benefit from the Earth experience. ~ We would urge you not to waste time on such matters, but to accept who you are – as you are – and use your energy to extract the last drop of teaching from your experiences. ~ We also suggest that you sit and meditate on those events in your life that cause you concern. ~ You will find all the answers that you need when you are quiet and listening to your soul promptings. ~ The constant rushing about and the constant din of Earth life does not allow your inner-self to speak to you, until you set aside a period of quiet for contemplation. ~ We would also like to assure each one, that where you are is where you ought to be. ~ So again we say do not waste energy in wanting to live somewhere else. ~ Be content with your lot and offer thanks each day, for that is the only way you will learn from the tools you were given. ~ Do not envy others what they have, for they too have lessons to learn and you may not like their lessons; so we would suggest that your own lessons will suffice. ൿ We will assure you that when a lesson is learned you will move on. ൿ If this should mean that you change your place of living then you will receive the right impressions as to the next step. ൿ Those who follow the path that is for them will always receive Spirit guidance."

Verse 41

Themes

Colour · Low & High Vibration · Music

"Every thing you see or touch is in a state of vibration. Depending on its vibration will define what it is that you see. Your thoughts vibrate to a different level, which again depends on the thought that you are thinking; the higher the thought, the higher the vibration. ൿ When you meet someone for the first time, you know immediately whether or not you could feel in tune with that person and perhaps, be willing to meet that one again. ൿ This would indicate that *your* vibrations touched *theirs* and the feeling was compatible. ൿ When it is time to go into meditation, it is usual to raise one's vibrations to place thoughts on as high a plane as possible; the higher the vibration, the more relaxing and worthwhile that meditation will be. ൿ All colours have high vibrations and so has music, for music and colour go hand in hand. ൿ Each colour has a musical note and of course each musical note has a colour. ൿ We often have concerts in the World of Spirit so that we can enjoy the wonderful spectacle of the colour with music. ൿ Even the spoken voice in your world can show lovely colours when the voice is used properly with the thread of love to run through it. ൿ Because your inner-sight is not as sensitive as ours, you are not able to appreciate these beautiful aspects of life. ൿ When you come home to our world, you will learn and understand much that was denied to you while on Earth. ൿ

We would urge you to keep away from the harsh sounds as far as possible, for they are of a low vibration and will jar against your finer senses. ❧ Harsh voices tend to drown out the sweeter sounds of the kindlier ones. ❧ Nothing is to be gained from too much contact with low vibrations. ❧ If *such* work was to be *your* life purpose, you would have known from an early age and your soul would have received special protection for this work. ❧ We say, keep your own energy field as pure as possible. ❧ If you feel you are under attack then place a coat of protection around yourself; it is easy to do. ❧ Think of your whole self surrounded by a white light and the effect of low vibrations will not harm you."

Verse 42

Themes:
- Contentment
- Earthly Needs vs. Material Wants
- Greed
- Happiness
- Money

"We see so many on the Earth Plane who are not happy or even content, because they cannot have all the things that they want. Here we say 'want' not 'need.' ❧ These are very different meanings. ❧ The needs of each one may vary somewhat, but are the basic requirements to enable life to continue. ❧ There are many on the Earth Plane now who do not even have sufficient for their needs, while others have more than they need in every sense of the word. ❧ We are not saying for one moment that you should not have some of the 'extra things' that, from a purely physical point of view, make life a pleasure. In fact we often urge you to enjoy those things which you have. Even if you are wealthy then enjoy it while you are able, for it was given to you for a purpose, and that purpose is for you to discover or 'it' will be made plain to you. ❧ Those to whom we refer are those who are not satisfied with the things they have got, but always envy others *their* possessions. ❧ This is very destructive, because the thought of envy prevents the enjoyment and use of the things that are there, and in time even those things will be taken away. ~ The miser who continually adds up his money will find that he has 'nothing' because he cannot bring himself to use it for any purpose – even enjoyment. ~ If the nations of the Earth Plane continue to place so much importance to the power of money, there may well come a time when it will be swept away. ~ If that should happen the only means for survival will be the ability to serve or exchange goods for the needs of life. ~ Then money will have lost its grip on the world and a more spiritual understanding of 'true needs' will take its place. ~ We say be content with what you have. ~ Acceptance is the key to happiness, for all else will cloud what God has intended for each one. ~ Accept your lessons with good grace because *each* is a step on the way to the joy of union with the Godhead."

Verse 43

Themes:
- Balance: Mental
- Physical
- Spiritual

"We would like to say a few words about balance. ~ You may think that balance does not apply to 'things spiritual' but it is of great importance. ~ Those who care for their physical bodies try to make sure that the food taken each day is part of a balanced diet, in order that the body may remain as healthy as possible. ~ As part of this care you are also advised to take regular exercise to keep the body fit. ~ The brain needs mental stimulus to prevent *its* decline. ~ All this you undertake on a regular basis, but when it comes to 'things spiritual' this good practice does not seem to apply. ~ Take one who has been drawn into a church such as yours for the first time, everything is new and exciting and that soul goes away feeling exalted. ~ The effect is such that they cannot get enough of it and want to keep that feeling. ~ For a while, almost everything else in life is ignored in order to get more and more of this excitement. ~ Although this may be understandable it is also unhealthy. ~ We say *enjoy* the exalted state that comes, but take it one step at a time. ~ The normal activity of each week should include a visit to a meeting such as this, but must not be allowed to overrule all else. ~ If this is allowed to happen, a time will come when total confusion will take over and cause a mental block. ~ There is *no* competition, and the *slower* all the facts sink into the consciousness the better. ~ A happy life is achieved through balance of the physical activity of the body, stimulation of the brain and mind, and a healthy understanding of matters spiritual. ~ When the time comes that you are called home to Spirit, you will see all your life in the greatest detail – as we have said before. ~ Here *too*, a balance is struck between the good that was done in action or thought, and the not so good actions and thinking. ~ After evaluation of the life, there will be a bias toward good or not so good, and it is *that* bias that you carry over into your next incarnation. ~ In order that *all* things spiritual are slowly taken into understanding, it is wise to meditate on *all* that is new, so that your inner-self can fully realise its total effect."

Verse 44

Themes:

- Spiritual Evolvement and the Future

"Thought has to come before everything. ~ God created *all* that is by thought, and has allowed *humanity* to create by thought. ~ There is nothing that you wish to do that does not have a thought to come into your mind before you *do* anything. When you are thinking, you do not realise that the thoughts you are having are being given life. ~ Your mind is extremely powerful, but fortunately most do not realise the power that is latent within them. ~ If all did realise the extent of this power*, and discovered how to use it beyond the thinking stage, there would be an Earth Plane of chaos. ❧ It is sufficient for now that thoughts are powerful and do attain a life of their own; especially if the thought is persisted. ❧ The great brains of your world *do* have some idea of how to pursue the power they have in their minds and *do* bring about much good things, but even they cannot attain that next step in creativity, that is – so far – being withheld from Earth beings. ❧ When the Earth Plane has undergone many changes and its scientists reach a higher level of mind and spirituality, then the next step in creativity will be realised. ❧ All must wait until then, because although there are many now who have reached a higher level, it is the scientific brains that need to show they are worthy of the next revelation. ❧ Those of the Higher Realms must curb – to some extent – the greedy appetites of those who would lead the scientific community along the wrong path. ❧ The advances that will be realised in the Age to come *will* be worth waiting for. ❧ If you were to have them now and they were to be wrongly used or misunderstood, there would be *no* going back to before the knowledge came into being. ❧ One could not erase the past and start again. ❧ Once information has become available it cannot be taken away again. ❧ It is for this reason that the Higher Beings are waiting for those on Earth to acquire a more spiritual dimension to their thoughts and activities, before allowing further progress to be made."

Verse 45

Themes:
Feeling   The Senses

"In order to have knowledge of the Earth Plane you were given senses for you to sample that which is around you. ❧ In *some* people the senses tell a very limited story about the place in

* Personal Power – See Appendix – Note 2.

which they find themselves. ❧ It is almost as though there is 'disinterest' in their surroundings and therefore, the senses are not pushed to their limit so that more can be understood about the Plane that has been given to them. ❧ The physical senses are basic and to *our* heightened senses, very limited. ❧ With these senses you must acquaint yourselves with *your* world; learn from it and as far as possible enjoy all that you find. There is still much to enjoy and to marvel at, even if your senses are limited. ❧ However, you do have another 'sense' if it can be called that: it is that of 'feeling.' ❧ Quite often it is linked to the other senses but is really quite apart. ❧ Feeling will give you extra information. ❧ For instance, when *we* draw close to you, those who are sensitive will feel a presence. ❧ Some may *see* that presence but we are now interested in the feeling. ❧ This sense of feeling goes very deep within. ❧ When you are aware of love from another, it is 'the feeling' that you are receiving. ❧ Sometimes the feeling is so strong that you may be moved to tears. ❧ We have said – on several occasions – that when you are thinking about something that you do *not* wish to happen or *fear* may happen, the feeling is so strong that it can bring about the very thing you fear. ❧ If that depth of feeling could be put into the thing or situation you want so much, then it is more likely to occur. ❧ It seems to be a human failing that the things you do not want you get, because of this strength of feeling. ❧ Now that the Earth Plane has moved on somewhat since we were there, we would put feeling as an additional sense, and would place it ahead of the others because of the power that is with it. ❧ If you knew how to use it correctly you could move mountains; not that we would advocate such a feat. ❧ It is the feeling that you can summon, that affects the subconscious part of you. ❧ That part is so little understood, and perhaps it is just as well for all your sakes. ❧ So much mischief could be brought about by anyone whose spiritual level was not of the highest. ❧ When you use your sense of feeling, you will find your Earth experience far more rewarding and the lessons more easily understood."

Verse 46

Themes:
Day of Judgement   Judging Others

"As we have said on many occasions, you incarnate on the Earth Plane in order to learn from the experiences that the Earth Plane can teach. ~ There are some who may not need to return to your world unless they have a particular reason for doing so. ~ Therefore we want you to realise that *all* who are in incarnation at this moment are as imperfect as are you. ~ **That is why no-one should pass judgement on another.** ~ Remember, *all* your thoughts and actions are known; for nothing can be hidden, even if your activity can be kept from mortal view. ~ Some are concerned about the Day of Judgement. ~ We prefer to call it your 'life review' but it should not cause fear or distress. ~ You will not be required to face your review at the moment of your passing to Spirit. You can choose your own time for this experience – when *you* feel ready to face *yourself* – for that is what it is. ~ It is rather like seeing your whole life played before you with all your thoughts as well as your actions shown in great detail. ~ Not only that, but *how* your thoughts and actions affected those with whom you came in contact. ~ It is a very serious time and the experience is akin to being totally exposed in all your frailty. ~ It is then that *you* judge yourself harshly; much more so than another may judge you. ~ If it was another, you would expect to receive some degree of mercy, but you show yourself no mercy whatever. ~ It is for *this* reason that *you* judge yourself. ~ There are some who cannot face that day and seeing themselves as they really were. ~ That is *their* choice, but they cannot make any progress in the World of Spirit because they have no tools with which to make that progress. ~ They stay where they find themselves. ~ They will receive much counselling and after a period, some will agree to the review and then progress can begin. ❧ If you cannot face up to the mistakes you have made, you cannot expect to make any progress; for it is from the mistakes that *true* understanding begins and humility finds a welcome place in the soul."

Verse 47

Themes:

- Change
- Fear
- Life Plan

"The essence of life on the Earth Plane is change. ❧ Change is a *necessary* part of growth, and growth *is* progress. ❧ For many, change brings fear. ❧ Some yearn for change from a current situation but for others it can mean loss. ❧ For one who has facial beauty, there is fear that the advancing years will veil that beauty. ❧ Some have *all* that wealth can bring and yet fear change, for within it they may lose everything. ❧ When life feels good and the path ahead looks straight and easy beware, the appearance of anything can be deceptive. Most of you will have found from experience that you can carefully lay plans for the future but there is no guarantee that those plans will come to fruition. ❧ If the 'life path' *does* fit in with a human plan then instinctively that soul is in tune with Spirit. First and foremost, you visit the Earth Plane in order to learn many lessons, and 'human plans' do not always fit in with those lessons. ❧ If you make an effort to understand this, and realise that change *must* be taken into account when any plan is laid, then you will be cooperating with your 'spiritual path' and find that disappointment will not visit you as often. ❧ It is *when* humanity is in conflict with the necessary experiences of life, that there is anger and bitterness towards life; this need not be so. ❧ Although each one is given free will, this does not mean that the pursuit of pleasure is the only reason for life. ❧ Each one agreed to a framework of learning before the life was awarded, and it is within that framework that free will can be exercised. ❧ Essentially, once adulthood is reached, then the individual should have felt the promptings of the correct life path. ～ Once this has been understood and followed, then the framework of that life is in action. ～ The filling in of that total picture is governed by the individual free will, and the giving of service to others should be a part of each one's joy of living. ～ To find your own path – if you have not yet found it – ask Spirit for help and then meditate upon it."

Note: Read Verses 48 & 49 in conjunction with this lesson.

Verse 48

Themes:

Incarnation* · Parents · The Framework

"We have already referred to the framework that is put into place before you incarnate on the Earth Plane. ～ We will take this matter in more detail because we feel that there are some who may not understand what it is, and how it operates. ～ When the time comes that you wish to incarnate again – because you feel that you need more Earth experiences, or that you have been advised to do so by the Wise Ones – there has to be a time of preparation. ～ We have said on many occasions that nothing is by accident, and all occurrences are in place by intention. ～ It may not appear in that light to you – who are in the midst of it – but if you were to stand back and be able to take the broad view, you would understand what we say. ～ To obtain the greatest benefit from an incarnation there *has* to be a plan of action. ～ This is what we call 'the framework'. ～ If your previous life on the Earth has enabled spiritual growth to take place, the Wise Ones look at the spiritual experiences as well as the physical experiences and can see where further growth is needed. ～ We hasten to add here that during this time, you are not left out of the discussions, for it is *your* development that is under consideration. ～ They point out your weaknesses, and the type of experiences that are required

* See Appendix – Note 1.

to give the strengthening and growth that is advisable to be able to progress further. ❧ That is not the end of the discussions. ❧ Suitable parents have to be chosen in order to start that soul on the road of those experiences. ❧ In fact, armed with the necessary knowledge given by the Wise Ones, *you* select your parents – with advice of course. ❧ Each of you belongs to a fairly large group, and it is usual that your choice of parents come from that group, but it is not an unbreakable rule. ❧ Once the choice is made, then the correct time of birth into the World of Matter is decided upon. ❧ The time is most important because the hour of the day, the day of the week, and the month of the year, each exert influences upon that Spirit incarnating. ❧ These influences will assist or hinder the spiritual development. ❧ At another time, we will explain some of those influences."

Note: Read Verses 47 & 49 in conjunction with this lesson.

Verse 49

Themes:

Astrology   Natal Chart*

"We said we would tell you why the birth time is important. The correct time of the birth was decided upon because *that time* would attract the right influences. ❧ Most people are not aware that you are surrounded by vibrations reaching the Earth Plane from a large number of sources; some of these influences are benign but some should be avoided if at all possible. ❧ Remember too that the Mother of the incoming soul is also influenced by these rays of energy. ❧ It is the Wise Ones who decide the correct time, so that the beneficial rays will help the incarnating one to find the correct life path. ❧ The efforts of the Wise Ones will be frustrated when human doctors – who think they know best – alter the time that the birth takes place to suit their own arrangements. ❧ This act can have a

* See Appendix – Note 1.

detrimental effect on the life of that soul. ~ Medical intervention can prevent those beneficial rays from reaching *that* soul at *that* significant time. ~ Each one of you was born under the main influence of a colour ray, as well as the myriad of other vibrations that were bombarding the Earth Plane at that particular time. ~ There are rays or vibrations if you prefer, that come from the planets in the solar system. ~ Some of these are very good, but some – at certain times – will hinder the one under which the birth took place. ~ The Moon sends her rays very strongly because the Moon is so close to Earth, but there are times when this influence will hinder the new soul. ~ It is a study which should be undertaken in depth by those who have an interest in the subject, and not dismissed as irrelevant. ~ Everything on the Earth Plane emits vibrations and therefore will influence everything else. ~ As is already understood, some of these influences will repel as well as attract, so great care is taken with the birth timing. ~ A birth brought forward because of an emergency, would have been allowed for in the planning. ~ In spite of the technical advances of human kind, there is a vast array of knowledge of which – so far – humans are totally unaware."

Note: Read Verses 47 & 48 in conjunction with this lesson.

Verse 50

Themes:

- Life in the World of Spirit

"There have been many descriptions of life in the World of Spirit as well as its scenery. ~ Many of these accounts seem to conflict one with another. ~ On the face of it, the conclusion of those who read these accounts is that they are untrue, but this is not so. ~ We wish to remind you here that our world is similar but very different from the Earth Plane. ~ The accounts that you read are true but they relate to the lower astral in many cases. ~ This is a plane of the familiar. ~ The newly arrived needs to be comforted after the experience of passing for which often the soul is unprepared. ∾ That soul feels at ease to see familiar sights, and he quickly finds that he can have what he wants. ∾ For those who feel that a cup of tea is what they need, a cup of tea is what they get. ∾ While still in the physical body, most will dream of the things they would like to have if the means were available, or the type of house they would like to live in. ∾ It may not have been possible for these dreams to be fulfilled during the Earth life, but they can be fulfilled in the World of Spirit. ∾ When they have completed the review of their recent life and repaid what has been possible to repay, or agree to put right, then they can begin to realise some of their longed for dreams. ∾ The dream may not be for a dwelling at all but for further education where it was denied them on the Earth, or they may wish to study art or music. ∾ There are many secret longings that can never be satisfied until arrival in the World of Spirit. ∾ Now perhaps, you may understand that if you ask any one of these people of life in Spirit you will often get an account of their dream fulfilment, though they would not see it as that. ∾ When a soul has satisfied these very real needs and begins to rise above the astral planes then you will get a very different interpretation of Spirit life. ∾ It is *then* that true progress has begun; it is *then* that the soul hungers for wisdom and understanding. ∾ There is nothing wrong with the needs as we have described for that is part of soul experience. ∾ Study in depth of any subject – which appeals – is encouraged, because then help can be given to those on the Earth. ∾ Service is the currency of achievement in the World of Spirit."

Verse 51

Themes:

- Death
- Masters
- Spirit and the Earth Plane

"Most of you have already accepted that there is no death in the usual meaning of the word, but at physical death the soul of the individual is released to return to the World of Spirit. ∾ Many wonder where they go; where that place is. ∾ We can tell you that with the transition, there is a change of consciousness. There is little change of place, for the soul is still within the aura of the Earth Plane. ∾ All that lives has an aura. ∾ When there is *no* aura, there is *no* life. ∾ The Earth is very much alive and suffers greatly at the hand of humankind and its ignorance. ∾ The limitations of the physical life on Earth prevent most from any understanding of this. ∾ Some are able to 'see and know' beyond the five senses, but even then, do not really appreciate that the Spirit World is so very close to the Earth and is greatly affected by the influences of the Earth. ∾ It may take a very long time in Earth years before a soul has progressed far enough to rise beyond the Earth's aura to planes of consciousness far beyond your present understanding. ∾ To fully understand something, means that the individual has reached that level, and there are few on the Earth who do understand those Higher Levels and the great work that has been entrusted to them. ∾ Those beings are known to you as Masters, and although there are Masters in incarnation at this time – for special purposes – they are, as we have said, few in number. ∾ You may at this point, wonder why we refer to a being as 'Soul' rather than 'Spirit?' ∾ All is Spirit at its core; but Spirit is pure light and as such could not function in the lower planes. ∾ The Spirit has to be covered for its protection and for that reason we say soul. ∾ Those beings who reside on the Higher Planes are pure light; the more advanced the being the greater the intensity of light that is given for the benefit of all. ∾ It is God's light and glory that streams forth from the sun and without it you would cease to be."

Verse 52

Themes:

The Power of Thought · Wrong Thoughts

"In our words to you we often refer to the importance of thought. ∾ Again we want to stress to you how important 'thought' or the type of thought is. ∾ Before any action can begin there has to be a thought or even many thoughts about it. ∾ It may be the materials required to bring your thought into being. ∾ It could be the composition of a very special letter or the application for a new job. ∾ Whatever it is that is to done, thoughts have to precede it. ∾ There are many who spend most of their time in thinking about what they would like to do if only they had the money – but achieve little. These thoughts are harmless enough but there are those who spend their time thinking of ways to get more of life's good things without the need of working for them. ∾ These souls do not understand the goodness of life in general and the huge numbers of people who make an effort to lead useful lives. There are some who think that just thinking is all right so long as the things thought about are *not* carried out. ∾ This is wrong thinking! ∾ The thought has already created the outline of the thing in the ether, and if the thought has been about another person and was very unkind, or was 'the thing' you would say if you saw them again, then the damage has been done. ∾ Harbour no ill thoughts of others for they will return to you in double measure. ∾ All the while you are in incarnation, all *good* thoughts and actions make a place for you in the World of Spirit. ∾ When you pass to Spirit, you will be drawn to the area which will reflect the thoughts and actions of your Earth life. ∾ Depressing thoughts or thoughts that are envious and greedy will find their creator among like-minded people in an equally depressing area. ~ We urge you to spread light and truth and reap the reward in your Spirit life to come. ~ Blame no-one for the lessons along the way, but find God's peace within your own being. ~ Ask for courage and upliftment each day and Spirit will never fail you."

Verse 53

Themes:
- Charity
- Giving
- Loneliness
- Service
- Volunteering

"When you give to a charity do you give spontaneously and with love? ~ Do you give it with a blessing that it will do the most good in the relief of suffering? ~ Even if your gift is small, if it is sent out with love it will find its rightful home. ~ No gift should be sent as an insurance policy hoping to buy yourself a better place in the World of Spirit. ~ Spiritual love and compassion for the needs of another is entered on your passport to the World of Spirit. ~ It is not always money that we speak about; the gift of your time to another who is perhaps lonely or needs a helping hand to ease the burden of life, is just as valuable as money, in fact we would say even more so. ~ To give money is comparatively easy because it does not involve the giver in further commitment, but the gift of time and understanding of another's needs is true service. ~ So often we refer to the giving of service but it is *so* important. ~ If each one were to give service in some form there would be many more people who would look on life in hope. ~ Too many are sad and lonely people who would benefit from an occasional visit to enjoy a cup of tea and a chat. ~ In that type of human contact there is healing taking place. ~ Even one hour of your Earth time once a week could make such a difference to one who is lonely. ~ We do not intend these words to sound like preaching but we are aware that some feel there is nothing they can do. ~ There is *always* something that one can do for another. ~ We will help with the right words where the situation is difficult, but if there is the desire to help, then help can be given. ~ As we have said, little acts of kindness can be given to others even if you cannot give money. ~ When money no longer has any meaning or value, the only coin will be the willingness to help each other without the expectation of repayment. ~ Many will have to rethink their values when there is nothing left except a loving heart and the desire to give service where it is needed."

Verse 54

Themes:

Laughter   Raising Your Vibration

"When we speak to you about becoming more spiritual in your thinking and behaviour, we feel that some of you may think that to make such ideas 'your own' would in some way restrict you. ~ You feel that to live on the Earth Plane is to enjoy life as far as possible and to worry about the next Plane of life when it comes. ~ To some, a spiritual life means taking all things very seriously and walking through your days with a glum countenance and generally trying to feel holy! ~ This is so far from the truth. ~ There is much fun and laughter in *our* world and why should it not be so? ~ Laughter raises your vibrations and your capacity to live. ~ Laughter is the tonic of life, wherever life is to be found on all the Planes of Spirit. You were created in love, light, truth and joy, so why not be happy while you are learning to understand more of Spirit? Your pathway through all the Planes of knowledge and understanding is a long one – which does eventually lead to perfection. ~ It was intended that you should enjoy the journey. ~ If you should lose the capacity for enjoyment, how can you appreciate all that your Father has to offer? ~ We do not mean that you should treat all spiritual matters in a frivolous way and belittle their impact, but to balance your times of study with a lighter touch. ❧ We know that some of the religions make their teaching rather heavy going with hardly any room for enjoyment, but *their* attitude should not affect *your* approach to spiritual thinking. ❧ In your daily meditations – when you are able to contact your Father within – they should give you that feeling of inner peace and quiet happiness. ❧ The more you reach this inner core of your being, the more you will understand what it is that we are saying. ❧ You will still have your lessons to learn, but the hardship they may bring can be tempered with that inner joy of overcoming and learning of the spiritual things that *really* matter. ❧ May your joy of life grow and shine through the darker patches."

Verse 55

Themes:
Expectations · Prayer · Responsibility

"There was a time – not too many years back – when the expectation of physical life on the Earth Plane was much shorter than it is now. ❧ Sons followed Fathers in their work ambitions and life progressed in an apparently ordered fashion. ❧ Since then education has been extended to all and because of it, ignorance of a persons talents has largely disappeared. ❧ Now, those with ability are encouraged to train for a more rewarding life. ❧ Because some are more gifted than others, there is a feeling that there is a 'superiority of person' because of these gifts. ❧ It has been said that those who have more to offer, more is expected of them. ❧ That is true of the World of Spirit. ❧ We find that those who have progressed to the Higher Planes, more is expected of them because the less able look to them for guidance and higher teaching. ❧ A large proportion of their time is taken up with teaching those on the lower planes as well as answering frequent calls from those on the Earth Plane. ❧ If we or any soul in the World of Spirit receive a request for help, it is never refused. ~ Think of the number of times you send a prayer to God for help over some problem or advice as to how to make the right choice in an important matter. ~ You expect some reply to your prayers and you will *always* receive help, but it may not be in the way that you thought it *should* be given. ~ On many occasions it has been realised that if you had received exactly what you had asked for, it would not have turned out the way you had expected and you may have been sorry. ~ For this reason it is best to make your request and leave the answer to Spirit, who can see a little further than you can at the moment that the prayer is sent to God. ~ The advice may not be that which you expect but is the right advice at that time. ~ A little later you will feel the urge to take a certain course, which will place your feet on the right path. ~ In times afar back, those souls did not have the expectations that you have now, and because of it could not enjoy the progress that is available to all who try to walk a spiritual path."

Verse 56

Themes:

- Christmas on Earth
- Christmas in Spirit

"At this time of *your* year you are preparing for many celebrations and as is said, a time for peace on your Earth Plane and good will to all. ~ Here we would ask a question: 'Why *now* that there should be peace and goodwill to all? ~ Why not at *all* times of the year?' ~ We have always found this strange. ~ Many go out of their way to find a warm and safe retreat for all who have fallen by the wayside and have no home to go to. ~ We ask you to think about making this effort all the year around, so that there are none who are forgotten and in need of this annual kindness. ~ We also enjoy this time of celebration though not in the way that you enjoy it. ~ We do not have special dinners or noisy parties but celebrate just the same. ❧ It is a time when we can go to our 'real home' which may be on quite a different plane from where we normally operate while being close to our charges on the Earth Plane. ❧ We go to our home where we can recharge ourselves and receive further instructions, and if necessary, further teaching. ❧ It is all very welcome because it is there that we are able to report on the progress of our charges and receive further advice on the future picture. ❧ We are also able to discuss *our* aspirations and how far we have progressed along our chosen path of service. ❧ It is all very happy and joyful to be with those whose friendship we value. ❧ It is here too, that we can bathe in the light from the Godhead, which is 'as food' for the Spirit. ❧ All our spiritual needs – at that time – are met, and we return to our tasks well refreshed and full of joy. ❧ We do not want you to think that as we go for our enjoyment too, that you are left alone. ❧ You are *never* left alone. ❧ If we are needed at this time we can be with you in a moment of your time. ❧ All the time we have promised to serve you, we have also promised that your needs come before our own – on every occasion – until our task is complete."

Verse 57

Themes:
- Contemplation
- Discernment
- Intuition
- Reflection
- Time out

"There are many occasions after a period of study, when it is felt that a little time on one's own to contemplate and go over some of the points of importance in the recent study time, would be an advantage. ❧ This is where the World of Spirit is truly wonderful. ❧ It is quite possible to choose the type of surroundings that would be perfect for quiet reflection. ❧ For those of you on Earth the need is the same, but the choice of quiet surroundings is not always possible. ❧ Within reason, we can have almost anything we wish to have and be anywhere we wish to be. ~ We can enjoy company or we can be alone. In our own home area, we are with those who are like we are and have made similar progress. ~ We do not have to worry about the integrity of those we meet for the first time as do you; we can see at a glance what they are like. ~ The robes we wear tell everyone we meet where we are on the ladder of progress and understanding. ~ You on the Earth Plane do not have this guidance and have to rely on your 'inner intuition' to act as your guide through the difficulties of Earth life. ~ We know that at every turn there seems to be others who would try to mislead the unwary into – sometimes – very desperate situations. ~ We can and do mix with such people but we do it from choice in trying to lead them away from the darkness of their own thoughts towards the light of understanding. ~ Sometimes we are successful but often, either they do not see us or turn away thinking we will make their conditions even worse. ~ They do not trust anyone because no-one trusted them while they were on the Earth Plane. ~ It is a joy to us when there is one who will turn to the light and is prepared to be helped. ~ It is then that they gradually come to understand the joys of Spirit; joys that were never to be found on the Earth Plane because of their mistrust of their fellow man. ~ Later they are to be found in deep study or in quiet contemplation, just as we were."

Verse 58

Themes:

- Intuition
- Compressed Time
- Disquiet

"For the last few years of your Earth time, those who are sensitive will have noticed that the vibration of the Earth is speeding up. ~ The reason for this is the need for a greater awareness of the influence of the Higher Beings who watch over the Earth. ~ Those incarnating now will have a different role to play in making people aware of Spirit and the need for a physical incarnation. ☙ Gradually all people will come to understand that each one is immortal and that an Earth incarnation is for experience and learning in order to make spiritual progress; then churches will be totally irrelevant. There will be the need for advanced teachers to lead doubters into belief and full understanding, but the teaching will be entirely practical and no-one will be told to have blind faith. The way of life will change with the change of thinking, but it will be a gradual process. ☙ If you will look around you and recall how life was a few years back, you will perhaps realise that the change is already taking effect. ☙ Time appears to pass more quickly than it used to. ☙ There is an unexplained rebelliousness and restlessness that was not in evidence in past time to the same degree. ☙ This is caused by those who are reluctant to move into what they believe is the unknown. ☙ It is not a conscious response, but their 'inner selves' wanting that which they have known before. ☙ It is also being caused by those who are more advanced – but finding no outlet for the elements of this spiritual change – want to tear down what they find, to force the change that they know is to be. ☙ In their impatience and frustration they are causing great fear and misery among the people. ☙ We do not condone their activity but want you to know there is a partial reason behind it. ☙ With more and more people turning to Spirit for guidance and teaching, they will realise that you do *not* get away with anything and in the end all actions must be accounted for. When this is understood by the majority then the problem of the tearaways will diminish."

Verse 59

Themes:
- Incarnation
- The Body and the Soul

"One of the greatest stumbling blocks to any spiritual understanding is the relationship of the physical body with the

Spirit – the Soul. ∾ As we have said before the body is not the real you. ∾ It may appear to be so because you are so accustomed to its use. ∾ It is a vehicle to carry your Spirit while you live in the World of Matter. ∾ Just as you will use your car to enable you to journey from place to place, so you use your body. ∾ You would not accept for one moment that the car was the real you because you can prove differently to everybody's satisfaction. ∾ We are now trying to tell you that your body has a similar function. ∾ In the same way that you care for your car so must you care for your body. ∾ The real you is pure Spirit, pure light. ∾ It is not the light that you can obtain from the use of a switch but the light of purity, which cannot exist in your world without a protective covering. ∾ You would not be able to look at it with physical eyes because of its brilliance. ∾ The Earth Plane is heavy and dark and your physical body is the most suitable clothing for the Spirit. The Spirit itself has received many coverings from its individualisation from the Godhead as it has passed through the many planes to reach its plane of teaching – which is the Earth Plane. ∾ Through the progress of many lives and experiences, each one will be able to dissolve one of the coverings of the Spirit. ∾ This is the progress that can be seen by those with Spirit vision because the spiritual light is that much brighter. ∾ As you are able to dissolve these finer Spirit coverings, so you will be able to rise through the planes of Spirit. ∾ You will now understand that there will come a point, when most of those finer layers have been dissolved, and you will not be required to return to the Earth unless you have a special task to perform that only an incarnation can be justified. ∾ Until the lure of the Earth Plane has lost its attractions, so will more lives be required."

Verse 60

Themes:

♨ Dealing with the Past ♨ Living in the NOW

"We want each one to find happiness while on the Plane of Earth. ~ This may sound too good to be true but it is possible; it only requires a change of thinking. ~ First of all you must realise that you only have NOW – this moment. ~ You must be aware of now and live within it. ~ You cannot be certain that you have tomorrow in which to place today's activities. ~ You may not have tomorrow or next week in which to do those things you have put aside. ~ What needs to be done, do now or today; do not put it off. ~ By this same understanding you must give up worrying about yesterday, last week or last year. ~ You *cannot* change any part of any activity or any mistakes that you may have made. ~ Not even one second of the past can be changed so why go over it again and again? ~ In so doing you are placing an unnecessary burden upon your shoulders. ~ If it is the consequence of those mistakes that you are worried about, then you must do all that is within your power to put it right. ~ It can be done by admitting your failure or error to those affected, and giving some service as a token of your sincerity. ~ If you cannot find the courage to put matters right then you condemn yourself to carrying that burden of guilt for the remainder of your earthly life. ~ Those who cannot let go of the past are carrying a burden of guilt. ~ We do not suggest that you forget the memories of past times; we only refer to those who continually go over past wrongs – either real or imagined. ~ Ask for help from your Spirit Helpers and they will guide you along the correct path *if* you can find the time to sit quietly and listen to that small voice that will make itself known. ~ If you can do as we have suggested, then you will be conscious of a release and a lightness that you may not have felt before. ~ It is *then* that a feeling of inner peace and happiness will fill your being."

Verse 61

Themes:
Balance · Happiness · Materialism · Meditation · Positive Thinking

---

"Once again, as we draw close to the vibrations of the Earth Plane, we are aware of the depth of unhappiness within most people. ~ Even when there is all that could be desired materially, there is unhappiness in the centre of being. Material possessions do not bring either peace or happiness; the 'inner soul' requires something more than just the gratification of the senses. ~ Meditation will help; but what type of meditation? ~ It is of no use just to sit and drift into some kind of dream exploring a wish list. ~ True meditation is mental work and requires effort. ~ Keeping the mind focussed on a specific subject is hard work for those who are not accustomed to mental discipline. ~ If you wish to change your life for the better you must change your thinking. ~ We can assure you that if you are prepared to give up a little of your time and accept mental discipline you will succeed. ~ Ask for help from Spirit each time the exercise is undertaken. ~ To set the right mental attitude, we suggest that you offer a prayer of gratitude for all that you have. ~ Be conscious of the things you *do* have and *do not* include material possessions. Such things may be with you today but could just as easily be gone tomorrow. ~ Be aware of the beauties of Nature, of friendships and all the things you appreciate that cannot be purchased. ~ These things inspire gratitude and should be dwelt upon mentally. ~ There should be the desire within each one, to be used to bring help and healing to those in need. ~ When you are conscious of the many blessings and gifts bestowed upon you, your Spirit should start to soar upwards; it is then that you are ready for your meditation on whatever is your chosen subject. ~ We advise that you should *not* bring the lack of anything into your meditation. ~ If you *do*, not only will you negate your meditation but, you invite more of the things you *do not* want! ೋ Your mind is a powerful tool so it should be used with wisdom. ೋ Always use positive thoughts in every area of your life and banish negative thoughts from your mind."

Verse 62

Themes:

Choices · Right Choices · Wrong Choices

"Each day you are required to make choices. ೋ Mostly these choices are easy to make because they are made according to the needs of the moment. ೋ There are times when the choice to be made will affect others – usually the close family – and the individual is concerned whether it is right or wrong to follow one's personal choice, or to sacrifice that choice, for the feelings of the close family. ೋ This matter will occupy the thinking over a period of time and no satisfactory conclusion can be reached. ೋ A friend may be consulted and will offer advice as to how *they* would react if the choice was made by them. ೋ The friend is being as helpful as possible but the advice given is from *their* standpoint at that moment, and *their* level of understanding. ೋ All it will give is another point of view, but will not truly help the enquirer. ೋ All decisions must be made from one's own sense of responsibility and awareness of spiritual growth at that particular point of time. ೋ The answer must be given and at last a choice is made. ೋ The result is a series of experiences, which will bring benefit and a deeper awareness of life. ೋ Looking back much later as to the wisdom of the choice that was made, it may be realised that it was the wrong choice. ೋ Perhaps the path was hard and not at all how the prospect turned out. ೋ It would never be known how the future would be *if* a different choice was made. It is easy to be wise afterwards but a choice had to be made. ೋ We say that there is no right or wrong choice but that the choice is made with the understanding of that moment. ~ Each one does the best that can be done at the time, but even if the wrong choice has been made valuable lessons have been learned. ~ The Spirit has grown as a result of the experiences that were undergone; and with a deeper understanding of life – and at a later time – a different choice would be made, then it would be the right decision. ~ However life appears to turn out for you, the Wise Ones ensure that there is growth spiritually in *all* choice, even if the individual is reluctant to admit it."

Verse 63

Themes:
Giving · Love · The Power of Thought

"The misery and unhappiness that beset many on the Earth Plane today is entirely a creation of the human people. ~ This may be an unacceptable statement if you are one of those who are suffering; however it is true. ~ When you were created by God out of Himself you were a perfect, shining spiritual being. ~ You understood nothing but Love because you were created out of Love by Love. ~ You were carried through the many Planes of Spirit – each giving something of their knowledge – before being ready for incarnation into experience of the school called Earth. ~ Gradually your perception of all that had gone before became clouded, and this state of perfection was placed further into the background. ~ Your Earth training had begun but not the training that had been envisaged by the Great Ones. ~ It was too late to prevent further Earth Plane incarnations so the change in the perception of perfection was allowed to continue as a form of training. ~ Many civilizations came and went and the peoples learned very little overall, but progress was made up the spiritual ladder, mainly through misery and desperation. Remember, 'thoughts' are things. ~ If you expect the worst to happen it will, sooner or later. ~ If you mistrust another you will find a reason for that mistrust. ~ If however, you extend unconditional love to all, love is what you will find. ~ It is your perception of the situation that will govern the outcome. Those who expect to find evil or hostility will indeed find it, which will in turn lead to further breakdown of understanding. This is how a warlike situation is started. ~ Those who find something unpleasant in another – without just cause – are merely finding a reflection of themselves. ~ Those whose lives are seeing beauty on the dullest day, and fill their time with thoughts of love for others, and healing for the less fortunate, will find inner peace and their needs filled. ~ Your thinking controls your outer experience. ~ If you want to have the good things, you must want others to have those things before you, and to feel their joy at receiving them. ~ Give out happiness and love even if you are suffering at this moment, and you will find your life turn around."

Verse 64

Themes:

- Ascension
- Judgement
- Karma
- Spiritual Growth

"From all sides you are advised not to judge another in any way whatsoever and this is very good advice. ~ Your human standpoint seems to bring judgement on those you meet without any intention of being unkind. ~ Often we hear quite complementary remarks about others but it is a form of judgement however innocent. ~ It is best not to get into that habit – even kindly – but to get out of commenting on others. If there is something unpleasant about another then the best you can do for that person is to send out your thoughts of love and upliftment to them. ~ If this is done with care, then in time, this love will be felt and a change of thinking will occur without their bringing it about consciously. ~ We know this is very difficult to achieve and it will take one who is of saintlike character to be able to be non-judgemental. ~ We say this to you because whatever you do or think that in any way affects another, will rebound upon you at some time in the future. You are responsible for all that you think, say and do throughout your life. ~ We want you to think quietly about this. ~ The time will come when you must face up to all that you have done. ~ We are sure there will be many good works that you may have forgotten about, but there could also be much that you would wish had not taken place but then it is too late, and amends will have to be made. ~ It is more difficult, once you have returned to Spirit, to make amends for wrong thinking and wrong actions but still it will have to be put right. Until the slate is wiped clean, as the saying goes, there can be no progress to a Higher Plane. ~ The purpose of the many incarnations that all must go through is to eventually reach the Godhead as a complete soul experienced in all the wisdom of the spheres. ~ The Plane of Earth is not the only plane of experience and incarnation. ~ It is for that reason that you have eternity to achieve the highest. ~ As your wisdom increases so will your love of others increase."

Verse 65

Themes:

- Peace
- Religious Division

"In recent days* there has been much talk of peace and some would even say they want peace at any price. ~ We would like to remind you here that peace is not a commodity that can be bought or sold. ~ True peace must begin within each one. Each one must establish their own inner peace before they can extend the hand of friendship to those they were formerly in disagreement. ~ It is a difficult task for all who call for peace

* Given on 12th April 1998 and refers to the troubles in Northern Ireland.

without the understanding of the part they must play in it. Where there are divided communities, thoughts and words of hate have been sown for many years and to undo all that will take time. ೋ Lip service itself will not establish that which they desire. ೋ It is all the more sad when the conflict is over religion. ೋ The root of many conflicts is religion and we find it difficult to understand when those at war profess to worship the Supreme Being you call God. ೋ It seems to us that the cause of conflict is the method and rituals of that worship. When the rituals are entirely man-made and were not ordained by God then we can understand why there should be such intense hatred. ೋ Remember, it is good to meet and discuss the difficulties of each and understanding the other. ೋ In the World of Spirit we do not always agree with others on every matter. ೋ We accept that each is an individual Spirit entitled to individual thought. ೋ We are all at a different stage of development and evolution and it would be an impossible task to expect all peoples on the Earth and in the Spirit World to always agree on everything. ೋ Each one will express themselves from their *own* point of consciousness. ೋ We would remind you also that no one on the Earth Plane is perfect, and because of it, there is bound to be differences of opinion. ೋ **Peace is an accommodation of various opinions.** ೋ It will take time to heal the hurts of the past but around your world an effort *must* be made. ೋ See in each one the spark of the Divine and that will bring peace to all who seek it within."

Verse 66

Themes:
- Negative Thinking
- The Brain
- The Mind

"If you damage your brain you will damage your life on the Earth Plane. ೋ It would be impossible to carry out the work that you agreed to do before you came into incarnation. ೋ It is the brain which is the computer and interpreter of all activity on the Earth Plane. You all know where the brain is situated but no-one can tell you where the mind is! The mind is the spiritual motor of each individual; for it is the *mind* that 'thinks' the thought that will pass on that thought for action. Before any action there has to be a thought; it is the mind which is responsible for it and the detail that will follow. All the while the mind is doing these things the brain is taking it as a blue print for action. The mind is the essential link with the Godhead; it is *that* part of God in humanity which is never separated from the Godhead. While there is life on the Earth Plane there is no separation from the energies that flow from the Godhead. That feeling of separation that many experience, especially in times of difficulty or trouble, is the result of negative thinking. In fact there has been no change; the flow of energies and love – which is also an energy – continues unabated. When next you find yourself facing a mountain of difficulty, make yourself stop for a moment and realise that those spiritual energies you receive each day, you need even more now; so a positive line of thinking is needed to solve the problems. This realisation will bring a sudden inflow of these energies with added strength to enable you to see your way through that which you are facing. Do not be tempted to fall into the negative trap, which is the easiest course of action to take. Do not be led along the wrong path. Make sure that your mind sends the correct message to your brain for action. Draw down to yourself God's love and blessing, and *that* will help smooth the path to a solution. It is the attitude to life that makes all the difference. When you have learned to solve your own problems this way, you will be well placed to help others to do the same."

Verse 67

Themes:
Balance · Material Life · Spiritual Life

"Every life on the Earth Plane will find difficulties that must be overcome. ∾ An Earth life is one of experience and learning. You will find that it is also a life of balance. ∾ We have spoken of this before and it is *very* important. ∾ In all your dealings in your material life balance is essential; for once things are out of balance, it is difficult to set the situation on the right track once more. ∾ When goods are being weighed, a balance of weight must be struck or there will be too much or too little of the item being weighed. ∾ If a worker is required to work too many long hours without sufficient time for rest and relaxation, then he will become ill because of it. ∾ The health of the body *must* be a balance between food, rest and exercise. ∾ If these conditions are not met, then health will break down and enforced rest will be required. ∾ Most illness is a breaking down of the balances in the body. ∾ The body is a very beautiful mechanism; which does need great care throughout the years of its use *if* you are to benefit from your Earth life. ∾ It is not only in the 'material world' that balance is required, it is essential from the 'spiritual world' too. ∾ If you think that the spiritual is not so important then we want you to think again. ∾ We hope that you will want to make progress to achieve a higher spiritual vibration while the experiences of life on Earth are available to you. ∾ We do not want you to think that the spiritual can wait until you are in the Spirit World before you need to concern yourself with it. ∾ You are Spirit here and now, and all you do will have a bearing on your manner of progress. ∾ It is for this reason that we want you to be aware of your spiritual life, and to be conscious of those who would help and inspire you to give that balance between the material and the spiritual. ∾ If you look upon it as irrelevant while on the Earth Plane, then you will find yourself unable to accept the World of Spirit when you find yourself in the midst of it."

Verse 68

Themes:

- Finding the 'Real' You
- Truth

"When you look into your mirror, is the image you see a true reflection of yourself, or do you see what it is *you* want to see? Do you create in your mind the image *you* wish the world to see and because of that 'mind picture,' it is reflected back to you? These are difficult questions to answer. ~ There are many on the Earth Plane who cannot select truth from untruth. ~ These are those souls who know deep down that their 'real self' is very flawed, and because of it do not wish the world to see it. These souls put on an act to cover themselves from those who *do* know truth from untruth. ~ However much they try to cover that which is unlovely, in times of pressure the real person can be seen. ~ The pressure of life is acting as a mirror to show the image that is usually kept hidden from view. Do not console yourselves with what you think you see or what you wish to see. ~ The truth will out sooner or later. ~ Do not rely on your mirror, but look into your 'real self' through meditation; see what is truly there and what needs to be changed. ~ When the day comes that you return to your home in the World of Spirit you will not be able to hide any part of yourself from the eyes of others. ~ All that you are will be known without the need of mirrors. ~ You have taken up an incarnation in order that you may discover the flaws in your own being. ~ There is not one soul upon the Earth Plane that does not need to face those flaws and know the way to overcome them. ~ First you must accept that you are on the Earth because you are imperfect. ~ Once accepted then learn to love. ~ Love with all your heart and in your loving, give out to those who are in need. ~ Your thoughts sent out in spiritual loving will repair those flaws and lead onto greater understanding of that road to perfection. ༄ Service is the giving out of this love in practical ways as well as in your thinking. ༄ The World of Spirit is a World of Love; it could be nothing less than Love."

Verse 69

Themes:

- Learning
- Progress
- Spiritualism
- Spiritual Growth
- Working with Spirit

"There are many of you who are attempting to uncover your gifts of the Spirit, so that you may serve and play your part in the giving of spiritual wisdom to those who are in need, and to those who also wish to serve but – so far – do not know how. ༄ Each one has a gift or ability if you prefer. ༄ It needs to be uncovered and trained as to its correct use *before* being demonstrated to those who are new to psychic gifts. ༄ To become a really good instrument for spiritual work may take several years, but it will be time well spent if the end result is to be of the highest quality. ༄ Too many are told they have 'an ability' and want to rush onto the platform – to demonstrate their gift – too early in their training. ༄ When this happens, true spiritual contact cannot be maintained because the channel has not been opened sufficiently to allow maximum access to the potential medium's gift. ༄ If each step is learned thoroughly, and the understanding between Spirit and the Medium is as close as is possible to achieve, then an element of trust can be built which will last as long as they both wish to work together. ༄ Trust between them is absolutely essential before any real work of importance can be done. ༄ If you are easily satisfied and will accept even a modest psychic ability, then you will only attract to you a Spirit Helper whose ability to work with you is 'adequate' but not of the highest. ༄ In *all* spiritual work, aim for the highest that you can reach, and you will attract to you one of similar quality. ~ We want you to remember that even in the World of Spirit all is not perfect and full of light as you may imagine. ~ If you were satisfied with good enough before you passed to Spirit then that same standard will still apply after you have arrived in the World of Spirit. ~ We have the 'mediocre' here as well as the highest and best. ~ Each one has to make the effort to progress out of the old ways in order to rise higher and even higher. ~ Life in Spirit is not a long holiday as you may have been led to believe. ~ Love and service is the currency here to achieve those things we are aiming for."

Verse 70

Themes:

- Absent Healing
- Ancient Powers
- Creative Thinking

"We want to draw your attention to thought. ~ Thought is most powerful if properly used. ~ We do not mean the idle thoughts that flow through the mind every passing minute, but intended concentrated thought. ~ If applied with care and consideration, it can produce beneficial results. ~ In absent or distant healing, it is the concentrated thought over several minutes that sends the healing energy to the one in need. ~ It has been proved that very great benefit has been received *even* when the distant patient has not been aware that healing energy is being given. ~ It has also been noted that *if* the patient knows the time of the thought concentration, and places themselves in a relaxed state of mind and body, a *greater* benefit is realised. ~ This just demonstrates that the one to benefit does not have to be present. ~ There is also a tendency for most people to visualise a situation that *may* occur, and think of the worst that *may* happen. ~ We wonder why it is that it is usual to see the worst first, before dismissing it and *then* to control the mind with a happier thought. ~ Those with a positive outlook will tend to think of the best most of the time, but there is always the little thought that something really unpleasant may happen. ❧ We want you to realise that *all* thoughts are things; meaning that the very act of thinking is creating that thing. ❧ Therefore to always think of the worst that can happen is creating it and inviting it to happen. ❧ When it does, there is a wail that 'what was thought' to happen, did happen. ❧ Of course it did, because the thinking constantly created it. ❧ Do not expect bad news about a situation but be positive and expect the best for everyone you know. Where there is collective thought – used in the right way – wonderful things can take place. ❧ In days before recorded history, the science of 'creative thinking' was used to build the most magnificent edifices. ❧ A group of dedicated craftsmen sat together and through creative thinking, were able to construct the most beautiful buildings. ❧ Every part was thought in detail together and bit-by-bit it became reality. ❧ We do not believe this could be done today because most would not dedicate themselves to the detail and more so, because most have a negative thought pattern. ❧ For this, absolute harmony is needed, and that is lacking in your world today."

Verse 71

Themes:
- Letting go of the Past
- Living in the NOW

"For a great number of people, the past is like a large amount of baggage, and worst of all, it must *always* be carried and can never be put down. ❧ That may seem like an exaggeration but it is an apt description. ❧ If for example, you had suffered at the hands of another or had undergone a very unpleasant experience, you would probably go over the event many times to judge the rights and wrongs of the situation. There is no harm in going over it in detail, to see what can be learned from it, but there is the tendency for it to become a continuous mode of thinking. ❧ It is then, that the events of the past become the baggage that cannot be put down, and tend to grow in size until they become excessive. ❧ If this does apply to any of you, we suggest you ask Spirit for help and make a determined effort to leave the past where it is and live in the NOW. ❧ Do not think in that way again. ❧ Live *this* minute and *every* minute in the NOW. ❧ Once an event has occurred, no amount of thought can change any moment of it. To live in the NOW allows you to control your future to a large degree, because *all* your thoughts and actions today will be carried over to affect your future. ❧ Live your days happily doing the best you can, and by placing your trust in Spirit to offer guidance when you need help over a problem. Remember to ask for that help when you need it. ❧ If things do not turn out the way you had hoped, then do the best you can with what you have got. ❧ With right guidance you may well find that appearances can be deceptive and the hopeless may turn out to be the best you could hope for. ❧ We want to help you turn despair into joy. ❧ There will be difficult times but with help you will win through. ❧ You are never asked to undergo an experience that you are not capable of learning from. ❧ When the lesson has been learned, there is always a period of peace and calm and the realisation of accomplishment. ❧ We ask a Blessing on all those who have earned their place on the spiritual highway."

Verse 72

Themes:
Prison   Spiritual Law*

"How difficult it is to live a 'spiritual life' in the world as it is today? ❧ There are so many rules that must be obeyed or suffer the punishments that may apply, according to the rule or law that has been broken, as well as the Spiritual Laws that apply to all. ❧ We agree that in order to live in peace with

* See Appendix – Note 3.

each other there must be laws for the good of the whole of that society ∾ In some parts of the Earth Plane the laws appear to be very severe compared to other areas. ∾ Where spirituality has diminished, materialism has taken over and the laws have become more difficult to understand. ∾ If humanity could begin to understand the Laws of Spirit *and* bring them into human law, then your Earth Plane would become the realm of peace which all are praying for. ∾ Now, when a person has broken the law and it is decided that a term of imprisonment is needed, that seems to be the end of it! ∾ Instead it should be realised that those who break the law of the land need help and education in understanding the necessity for those laws. There should be a great emphasis on education and proper training for a useful place in society. ∾ If this was done then God's Law would gain a foothold in that society. ∾ All who incarnate learn by example. ∾ A young child will copy and follow what he sees around him. ∾ He should not then be blamed for getting into trouble by following those who should be setting an example. ∾ God's Law is based entirely on love, because God is Love. ∾ You have been asked so many times to love others as you would love yourself. ∾ Similarly you have been asked to do to others, as you would have them do to you; again it is based on love. ∾ Those who are weak must receive help to help themselves, and by counselling and teaching shown how to balance a material world with the ways of Spirit. ∾ Only then can humanity hope to devise laws that will bring a kinder and more peaceful way of life for all."

Verse 73

Themes:
Honesty Integrity Rightness

"So often we have asked you to bring spiritual values into your every day material lives. ∾ Many have thought well on this, but have concluded that the material and the spiritual do not mix. ◌ If you think again, you will realise that the spiritual quality that we want you to include is of 'rightness.' ◌ In all your dealings, whether business or within the family, the element of honesty must be held up as the yardstick by which all is compared. ◌ If you are true to yourself and what you know to be the right way, then you are bringing the spiritual into your life. ◌ There is that knowledge deep within everyone as to what is right and true *and* the ways that should be avoided. ◌ Many may laugh at you for holding such notions saying they will cost you in the end. ◌ You may not gain materially from the way we urge you to adopt, but you will earn a clear conscience and will be following the Law of Love. All that pertains to universal love is the greatest Spiritual Law. If you do unto others as you would that they do unto you, you are following that Spiritual Law. ◌ The earthly rewards are not always as great, but when you return to the World of Spirit you will have less to account for if you had been kinder to your neighbours and your own family, and fairer in your dealings in your material world. ◌ The one who grabs all, regardless of how it is obtained may benefit in your world but think how it will be when he passes to this World of Spirit. ◌ He will carry a gloom with him, because he will have blotted out much of his spiritual light by his unloving methods in dealing with his brothers and sisters of the Earth Plane. ◌ The more he cheated them the less light he carried home to Spirit. ◌ We can assure you that for the short time you spend on the Earth Plane, it is not worth the misery of the burden of spiritual debt you would find on your shoulders on your arrival in the World of Spirit."

Verse 74

Themes:
Lessons Life Moving Forward

"Many words have been given to you about the World of Spirit and how we perceive your world at this time. ◌ We want you to realise that we willingly come to your world to help, advise and inspire. ~ We, who are just a little ahead of you, have also lived on the Earth Plane and know the difficulties and the temptations that beset all who agree to incarnate. ~ As we have said many times, those same difficulties and temptations are for teaching and strengthening *your* will to overcome those same difficulties. ~ We can help you through your hard times, but we cannot make decisions for you. ~ In order to learn you must be allowed to make mistakes, for that is the only way to learn anything of value. ~ You cannot learn the experience of life from a book. ~ Books are to add to your knowledge of a subject, but life is for understanding and an 'inner soul' knowing. ~ When life itself brings you up with a jolt and sets you to thinking: 'Why should this happen to me?' then we can inspire you with the thoughts that will take you further in your quest for the right answer. ~ However, if you are so taken down that you wish to wallow in your own misery then there is little we can do until you are prepared to sit quietly and listen, instead of wailing. ~ It is then that you will know the right words to speak at a given moment, or the right place to visit, or the right person to see. ~ If you allow these things to happen you will be amazed at the power of the help that is being given. ~ As we have said, the main framework of your life is laid down, but will only become obvious when you place yourself in a receptive mood in order to take the next step. ~ Those who want help with every step of the way will be disappointed, because once advice has been given and we know that it has been heard, it is *not* given again. ~ There are many who have decided on the words they wish to hear and will persist, consulting first one then another, hoping to hear those words. ~ We bring that which is right and helpful, but do not bow to idle wishes."

Verse 75

Themes:
A Better Life · Change · Greed
Materialism · Nature

"You are assailed* on all sides by those who want you to have all the material goods that you do *not* need, in order to satisfy *their* greed for greater profit. ~ Too much of Mother Nature's bounty is being squandered for no good reason and many of the Earth Plane's poor people have little. ~ This material way of life is causing many problems to many people and a cure for these ills is: a new way of life. ~ Material difficulties will increase – causing great despair and unhappiness for many – unless each one becomes aware of the beauty of Nature and turns away from the constant demand for more goods and returns to a simpler way of life. ~ The Great Spirit did not create the Earth Plane for a few to take all and give nothing in return. ~ The Earth is to be revered and its beauty maintained by each one, because you know that it was given to you for your well-being and understanding. ~ It was not intended that you should destroy it: to take more than you need is helping to destroy the thing that you love. ~ When we lived on the Earth Plane, life was primitive by comparison with what we see now, but we accepted it because there was nothing else. ~ We *too* had many problems but of an entirely different nature. ~ Our problems were with the Church, which was all-powerful at that time, and those who did not do its bidding found life very difficult and uncomfortable. ~ At least the people accepted God, even if they found 'that God' harsh and to be feared. Now it seems that fewer people accept God as the Creator of all that is, and prefer a 'material god' that will give them all the things they crave for, but do not need. ~ Their problems are great, and their sorrows are greater still, but they will not change their thinking. ~ Until each one discovers who they

* Assailed means attacked or assaulted.

really are, there will be no relief from the misery of today and tomorrow. ~ Stand back – look at your life – and see it for what it is, and resolve to do with less and to love more, before it is too late to make a difference in the future. ~ Remember, *your* thoughts and actions today will shape *your* future tomorrow."

Verse 76

Themes:
- Change
- Materialism
- Nature
- Religion
- The Past

"There are many problems that face each one on the Earth Plane at this time, but *do not* despair of solutions to those problems. ~ When *we* were living on the Earth Plane we too had many difficulties that were not easily overcome. ~ It was at a time when the Church was all powerful in the land; in fact even more powerful than the Kings at that time. ~ If a person did not comply with all the demands of the Church, then that one suffered greatly at the hands of the Church. ~ There was great ignorance in the masses and whatever the priests told them they had to believe. ~ We thought – at that time – that it was the Church alone that caused all the trouble, and to some extent it is true at *this* time but it now it goes further. ~ Then the power was religion but *now* the desire for power has moved to material things, and an even greater greed has reared its head. ~ Many more problems face the people of the Earth Plane than in former times. ~ At least then the mind of the people was centred on God even if 'that God' was a God to be feared. ~ Now, the mind of many people is centred entirely on things of a material nature, which at the same time is causing great damage to Mother Nature and before long, will cause untold distress to each one on the Earth Plane. ~ We urge each one to look within – in meditation – for the answer to each problem as you are aware of it. ~ You will overcome each problem as it confronts you but ask for the help you need. Do not force a way through your difficulty, for if you do, you will create further problems. ~ Try and observe it as though you were 'not involved' and you will see an opportunity to put matters right that would not have come into your mind before. ~ Always be aware that the old ways of doing things *have* to change, but first of all, each one must change themselves before they can help the world. ~ Look at life from a different angle and accept what you have with good grace until you find the wisdom to change it."

Verse 77

Themes:
The Self Your Life Plan

"Each one on the Earth Plane at this time wants to be happy. There is nothing wrong in wanting to be happy. ~ In fact it was not decreed that in order to learn of the Spirit, it must be done in misery. ~ Your God is a God of Love and wants each one to be happy and at the same time serving Spirit. ~ Your basic task is to know who you are, and in the knowing, to serve those around you and help *them* to know themselves and to serve. ~ Perhaps this sounds dull but in its realisation it will bring untold joy and happiness. ~ Each of you has a special part to play in the Plan of Creation as we have said before. ~ When you discover who you really are you will have found your path that you must follow in this incarnation. ~ You will know what your unique part is that you must play, and of course, it is something you must discover for yourself. ~ No-one else can tell you what it is, but when you have found it you will have found happiness. ~ We can say this with certainty because in 'the finding' you will have gone beyond 'self' and the self-seeking that most have interest in. ~ When you go beyond 'the self' a new perspective opens up before you and it is *then* you start a life of discovery. ~ No longer will you say to yourself: 'If I do that what's in it for me?' ~ Those mundane things which have their place under ordinary thinking suddenly have *no* meaning and *no* importance! ~ It is *then* that you have gone beyond 'self' and self-seeking. ~ You will find yourself totally absorbed in fulfilling the need that presents itself to you; that there is no room for personal thought or gain. ~ However, you will also find that quite without making the effort, your *own* needs will be met apparently without conscious thought. ~ This is the life that was intended for each one. ~ Meditate on finding the true self and the part you should play in God's wonderful Plan and you will find your life transformed. ~ Why pursue a way of pain and misery when happiness is around the corner?"

Verse 78

Themes:
Spiritual Development   World of Spirit

"The word 'progress' is a word frequently used and has come to mean many things to many people. ~ To one who is studying, it means the assimilation of knowledge in order to fit oneself for the next step on the chosen path. ~ For those in the world of business, it means moving towards a desired goal. For those of us in Spirit, it means so much more than anything the human brain can truly understand. ~ To us, spiritual progress is far removed from the usual activities of the Earth Plane. ~ You are beginning to realise that there is 'an understanding' that is spiritual, but your thinking does not fully grasp its meaning. ~ In meditation you *do* glimpse the spiritual, and many try to use this knowledge in their daily lives. ~ You make progress from a spiritual point of view when you learn the earthly lessons through experience, but that is not from choice but from necessity in order to get through the experience. ~ The spiritual progress we are speaking about is of seeking out the most desirable path to be aware of progress. ~ When you return to Spirit you will join groups of souls who actively seek knowledge in order to make the progress they so earnestly desire. ❧ There is discussion, and those who have gone a few steps ahead and wish to help, give much information. We are all each other's teacher, even as it is so on the Earth Plane. ❧ Those in these groups who are attentive will 'hear' that which they seek and can take it within their consciousness. ❧ It has become part of their being because they can really understand. ❧ True understanding is taking knowledge deep within the Spirit. ❧ It is as though that soul's spiritual light has received another ray of light and the whole shines more brightly. ❧ That soul's robe reflects this too, because the colour has changed or the pattern has altered in some way. ❧ It is the robe that all must wear that shows the exact state of that one's progress. ❧ There can be no pretence, for all is known whether it is good or that which causes shame."

Verse 79

Themes:

God · Judgement · Unconditional Love

"We remind you again and again to *love* with all your heart. We ask you to love God with every fibre of your being – first and foremost – and then *all* will follow in Divine order. ❧ There is nothing else but God in the whole Universe. ❧ There can be nothing outside of God for if there was, you would have to say, 'God and....' ❧ There is no 'God and...' there is only God Supreme, above all and in all. ❧ Every leaf on every tree was fashioned by God, as was every blade of grass. ❧ All was created out of 'love' itself. ❧ Even with this demonstration of love, humanity has difficulty in recognising and accepting this love. ❧ This 'something' we cannot understand. ❧ Many can accept that God created all the beauty of Nature, but when it comes to human form and the Spirit of God that lives within it, the difficulties of understanding seem to arise. ❧ The human form is nothing but a necessary cloak to enable the Spirit of God to live upon the Earth Plane. ~ When you look at another, you see the cloak and often judge. ~ Perhaps that cloak is not perfect in shape or is not as beautiful or as handsome as you would like. ~ We say do not look at the cloak only, but look for the Spirit within. ~ See the beauty of the Spirit that lives in that cloak. ~ Recognise that Spirit as another part of you, for we are all one in that Supreme Being we name God. ~ When you see the love of God in each one you meet, it is *your* love being reflected back to you. ~ This reflection of love will colour all you think and do. ~ If you will make that effort to see God in everything and everyone, your life will change for the better. ~ If others hurt you, send them your love, and in time *they* will begin to understand. Remember that you are a Spiritual being undertaking a life of experience on the Earth Plane. ~ When you are called home to Spirit you will see how far from love you strayed and how painful that straying was to be. ~ Whatever you give out in love, you will receive back many times over. ~ Whatever you send out grudgingly you will receive back grudgingly; that is a Law of Spirit that cannot be broken."

Verse 80

Themes:
Change · Earth Changes · Service

"Nothing remains the same. ~ Life on the Earth Plane brings change with it. ~ Some will say that their lives are dull and nothing changes but this is not so. ~ At the end of each day you are one day older. ~ The Earth Plane turns on its axis and speeds through space and it must continue to do so. That in itself brings changes in the seasons which affect everyone, wherever they live. ~ We who come close to the Earth are aware of these changes, and at the same time, try to impress the minds of men and women that the Plane of Spirit is hardly a breath away. ~ We want you to realise that as the season's change, so should your thinking also change, to bring the truth of Spirit into your lives. ~ It is no use thinking that it is all right to throw caution to the winds while young – and have a good time – and only start to think of spiritual matters when old. ~ We say why not combine spiritual thoughts and the spiritual approach to life while you are young? ~ It will not stop you having a good time. ~ In the Spirit World we laugh a lot and enjoy ourselves, for that does not stop us being what we are. ~ It is not dull and old-fashioned to be spiritual. ~ It means that you are aware that whatever you do or think must be loving and kindly to all around you. ~ It also means being willing to help those who need help or comfort when that need arises. ~ As the days pass, and those around you get older or sick, those changes may call upon you to offer what help you can. ~ It is being aware that 'change brings need' that those who are living a spiritual life will be able to fill. ~ The Earth Plane is also undergoing changes such as you are aware of at this time. ~ These changes will accelerate and much more will be required from those who are spiritually aware. ~ Those who are coming to maturity now will be the leaders as the Earth Plane renews itself and a kinder way of living emerges. ~ Your prayers and love will make a difference."

This reading was given on 15th November 1998

Verse 81

Themes:
- Earth Changes
- Spiritualism

"When you come into a spiritual movement such as this, much of what is said you will find an echo within you. ~ It is a 'knowing' that has surfaced from long ago. ~ Much of course of what you say is common sense, which – may we add – is *far* from common. ~ Once you hear the words, it is as if you have always known, and of course you have. ❧ In past time when you 'knew' you would not have dared to speak, because if you did, it was prison or the stake. ❧ Now the Earth Plane is more enlightened, but not enough yet. ❧ The time will come when questions will be asked that *your* understanding will be able to answer. ❧ That time is not yet. ❧ Your world has to suffer before that will come about. ❧ It could be likened to childbirth, the pain before the joy. ❧ We can tell you that the pain will be comparatively short-lived, but those that remain will know the joy of attainment. ❧ That attainment is 'the Peace' which has been spoken of for many years. ❧ We stress here that the peace of which we speak is not the absence of war, nor the giving-in to threats in order to prevent conflict. ❧ We speak of peace of the heart; of the willingness of each one to help another as the need arises, and to give comfort and love without the thought of repayment. ❧ Those are some of the ideals that we would wish to see take root on the Earth Plane. Then and only then, will your world begin to reflect some of the Light that is constantly sent from the World of Spirit. ❧ Your world is a dark place as it appears to us. ❧ It is cold and forbidding, and has a clinging dampness about it which would daunt all but the determined from coming too near. ❧ When the pain is over, there will be a crying out to God from the depth of the heart to end the suffering. ❧ Then we will be able to flood the Earth Plane with Love and Light, such as you have never known before. ❧ It will be *then* that true peace – which passes all understanding as of this moment – will take root among those that remain."

This reading was given on 29th November 1998.

Verse 82

Themes:
Adulthood · Balance · Children · Growing Up · Parental Responsibility

---

"Each time we bring our words to you, we try to show the way to be at peace with yourselves and find contentment from spiritual understanding. ~ Material things alone will not satisfy that deeper urge within you. ~ There must be a balance between the material and the spiritual – the mind and the body. ~ Extremes in all things are to be avoided. ~ As has been said in your world: 'A spoonful of a medicine will do you good, but the contents of the bottle may transfer you from your world to ours.' ~ When still a child you were the responsibility of your parents. ~ Once you attained adulthood you became responsible for yourself. ~ That means the new adults *must* make their own decisions. ~ They may ask 'those older' for advice on the matter in hand, but the final decision is theirs and once made, is *their* responsibility; and no blame for the result should be attached to anyone else. ~ This is where there is much misunderstanding. ~ The 'new adult' *must* be allowed to make their mistakes. ~ It is from making mistakes that true learning takes place. ~ Each adult is only responsible for their own growth and understanding. ~ It is good to receive advice and assistance from others *especially* where there is a difficult decision to make that will affect others. ~ There are *too* many parents who think that they should intervene in the affairs of 'their' so-called children, even when they are adult. ~ When mistakes are made, it is for their loved ones to gather round to show their love and understanding, and in so doing also know that that particular mistake will not be made again because they have learned from it. ~ There is no soul on the Earth Plane that has not made a mistake and 'hopefully' resolved not to go down that path again. ~ Remember that you are only responsible for yourselves and those under your care who are not yet adults. ~ You can take additional responsibilities for those with impaired understanding or who are in special need, but these are personal choices and come from a deeper spiritual understanding which is a topic for another point of discussion. ❧ At this time we stress this 'personal responsibility' because that too is a lesson in itself. ❧ So let well alone, and save any advice for when it is asked."

Verse 83

Themes:
- Christmas
- Giving
- Jesus
- Unconditional Love

"You are now approaching that time of your year when you show love and goodwill to each other ❧ Although it is supposed to be the celebration of the birth of the Master, this fact does not take up much thinking time for the majority of people. ❧ At this time of Christmas, each must take their own ideas about this very High Being. ❧ The main point that should come to the fore is the teaching that the Master brought to the world. ❧ That teaching revolved around the word 'love'. ❧ Whichever language you speak, that word or its equivalent exists. ❧ That is what He brought to the Plane of Earth 2,000 years ago in your Earth time. ❧ That word is sadly lacking from everyday life. ❧ The teaching and the meaning of that word was 'unconditioned love' – the love you should offer the stranger or your enemy, *if* you have any enemies. ❧ It is the love you should feel for *all* life, in whatever form it may manifest. ❧ You do not have to like the person in order to love them. ❧ God loves everything that has the spark of life within it. ❧ His love is not denied to even the smallest thing or to any member of the human population. ❧ If God, who knows everything of His creation, loves all that is within it, how can you deny your love for anyone? ❧ You send your greetings to many at this time of your year, but as soon as it is passed, you forget all that you said and revert to the way you were before the celebration.

When you send out love from the well of love within, you will see that love returned in many ways. ~ Similarly when you give to others in goods or money – in order to ease their burden – you should *not* do it in order to have some favour returned. ~ However, gifts given in this way are usually repaid in some other manner, at a time when *you* are in need of some help or upliftment. ~ We are pleased with the goodwill at this time but would like to see that love extended throughout each year. ~ May you be ever aware of God's Love as your constant companion."

Verse 84

Themes:
- Ancient Religious Texts
- The New Teachings
- Truth

"When we come to speak to you we bring our Love, Light and Truth. ~ The only difference from books of old, is that we bring 'that truth' up-to-date. ~ In whatever language you speak, truth must be the same. ~ The old way of expression and the old use of language have formed a barrier to the understanding of that truth, and that is why we bring that same understanding in words that we hope you will understand. Truth can never change if was truth in the first place. ~ If it does change over the years then it was not truth in the first utterance. ~ We have learned your language in order to properly give the right expression to that which we wish to say to you. ~ If you have listened carefully to our words, then you will recognise those same phrases – expressed in a modern way – in order to help your understanding. ~ We want you to let those words sink deeply into your being and use them as markers to take hold in times of difficulty, and those rough parts of your journey through your Earth life. ~ To comprehend our words it *does* depend upon your own point of understanding; in other words, where *you* are in the acceptance of spiritual matters. ❧ If you were to think that spiritual things are an 'extra' to your life, then you will not fully understand our words. ❧ You will hear them but you will not make them a part of your life and mode of living. ❧ If, for an example, you are unable to accept that God created all that is on all planes of existence everywhere, then we do not know how we can explain that fact in any other way. ❧ There are some limitations that language places on all who use it, but we have tried to bring truth into the simplest language that is possible to use. ❧ There have been many distortions of the truth, some has been deliberate and some has been through translation where the translator's ability was not adequate to the demands of the task. ❧ God loves all His creation, so do not blame God for the latest tragedy. ❧ Remember, He gave you free choice as to how you will follow *your* life, so when things do not go the way you wish, then perhaps you should look to your own thoughts or deeds first of all."

Verse 85

Themes:

- Change
- Letting go of the Past
- The New Year

"It is because we are close to the Earth Plane that we are aware that a 'new year' has begun. ❧ In the World of Spirit we do not have 'new years' because we do not have time in the way you do. ❧ We have our own festivals – which are allowed to coincide with your Christmas and Easter – to enable us to return to our true home and partake of the living waters that will spiritually strengthen us. ❧ We realise that a new year means a step into the unknown, but that is also true of each new day. ❧ This New Year time gives us an opportunity to remind you of love. ❧ We want you to take it into your thinking each and every day. ❧ Of course we do not speak of physical love but a spiritual love for every created thing. ❧

Love everyone you meet whoever they are. ❧ There is no need to demonstrate it of course, but to be aware that *they too* were created out of God's Love in the same way as you were. They too have their hopes and aspirations and it does not matter what their status is. ❧ They should be silently blessed, as *all* creation should receive a silent blessing each day. ❧ Now that you have your new year, allow a new way of thinking and close the door on the past. ❧ However you go over what *should* have been, none of it can be changed, therefore close the door on it and bid it farewell. ❧ Set aside the bitter arguments and regrets and send loving thoughts instead. ❧ As we have said before, you do not have to like everyone in order to love them, but love them you *must*. ❧ Provided you keep the door labelled 'past' firmly closed, you will begin to notice the difference and feel as if a heavy load is lifted from you. ❧ A new year should mean a 'new approach' to all that worries you. If love is brought into every-day thinking, you will soon find that your problems will more easily be solved, even if you do not believe it at this moment. ❧ Ask for God's Blessing on life and be determined in your heart that this *will* be a good year."

Verse 86

Themes:
- Connecting with Spirit
- The Spiritual Movement
- Vibration

"When you look around you, there is a tendency to feel secure because the things you see are solid. ❧ The chair you sit on supports you because it feels solid and so with all things on the Earth Plane. ❧ We can assure you that this feeling does not apply to us because we wear a different body – which is not composed of Earth matter. ❧ We can pass through your solid things and hardly be aware that they exist. ❧ It is all a matter of vibration. ❧ Everything is in a state of vibration. ❧ Your physical bodies vibrate in tune with the vibrations of the Earth Plane and therefore all Earthly things are solid to you. ~ We live in a faster vibration and our bodies are in tune with it and to us, 'it' is solid. ~ It is because we vibrate at a faster rate that you cannot see us with your Earthly sight. ~ Those who have the gift of clairvoyance are able to raise their vibrations to a 'higher rate' while we 'lower' ours so that the clairvoyant can see us and maybe hear us as well – using another gift, that of clairaudience. ~ The only time you are able to operate without realising it, is when you visit the Spirit Planes during sleep state. ~ There are some who will experience the apparent movement of articles such as photographs. ~ This is done to draw attention to those who still love you but live in a different world. ~ They want you to know that they are still very much alive and this is often the only way to draw your attention to them, by the movement of things or to bring a question to your mind. ~ To do this, the vibration must be stepped down, but *they* need help to achieve this. ~ We are happy to help because we know the pleasure it will bring when the loved one on Earth – at last – realises that death was not the end after all. ~ It is then that they may come to a meeting such as this and begin the happy journey of self-realisation. ~ Once they find that they will see their loved ones again, they come to know that Earth is but a preparation for something far more wonderful."

Verse 87

Themes:

- Effect of Thoughts
- Letting go of the Past
- The reason for *your* incarnation

"When we draw close to the Plane of Earth, we can see the 'mind workings' of the people. ~ We can also see the effect that those 'mind workings' have on the daily lives of each one. Areas of the aura which should be brightly coloured are made dull with the grey of worry. ❧ We look closer and see that it is the 'negative thinking' that causes this grey to descend like a veil around the one we are viewing. ❧ So many create a series of pictures – like a film – of what could go wrong in the situation under consideration. ❧ Those thoughts are powerful because they are negative and *will* create the event that is feared. ❧ These same persons tend to go over events of the past and by doing so *will* recreate those same situations again. ❧ There is no escape because they are continually thinking in this manner. Until this cycle is broken there is no release. ❧ The way to break it is to accept the past for what it was, and realize that though it caused much pain and anxiety it is finished. ❧ Going over it with phrases such as: 'If only I had done that instead or, if I had not said those words that would not have happened' is futile because you cannot change one second of your Earth time, however many times you go over what 'you believe' should have taken place. ❧ We urge you to accept it for what it was and resolve not to allow that situation to happen again. ❧ You are a little older and have learned from those mistakes. ❧ This is in fact the reason for your present incarnation, for how else can you learn a lesson except by living the experience? ❧ It is the resolve *not* to make those mistakes again, that you make the progress you were destined to make. By closing the door on the past and taking a positive outlook you will feel the veil of negativity falling away from you. ❧ Ask for strength from Spirit to help you in breaking the 'if onlys' of the past and go forward, knowing the light of Spirit will guide you."

Verse 88

Themes:
Young adults Spiritual development

"When you become an adult and take responsibility for yourself, you begin to paint a 'spiritual picture' of your life on the Earth Plane. ~ To begin with, the young mind sketches an outline of the way *they* wish their independent life to be. ~ It is then – with eagerness – that the painting is to begin. ~ At first all is well, and strong splashes of colour can be seen by those in the World of Spirit who inspire these newly responsible souls. ~ These souls are well prepared and are not so easily put off at the first opposition to their plans. ~ Even so, the painting comes to a standstill while the way forward is unblocked. ~ Perhaps the lure of the material world is too strong for that soul, and for a while no work on the spiritual picture is done. ~ The aspiring soul asks for help with an Earth problem and once more the chosen path is followed and the picture is continued. ~ It is in this manner that the World of Spirit guides you all, to progress toward the goal that was planned before the incarnation was undertaken. ~ There is no life that is easy and straightforward, for there is much to learn about the individual self that could never be learned in one incarnation. ~ It is not so much the learning about the self, but the reaction of others to the activities of the self in the course of this learning. ~ It is these reactions that change the picture that is being painted. ~ Very often, whole sections have to be taken out of the picture while that soul reassesses their progress to date. ~ Then, with a change of attitude, a better and more mature section can be inserted to show this complete change in understanding. ~ These changes come about when there has been a realisation of spiritual values as opposed to the current material attitude. ~ There is a wonderful feeling of knowing that lessons are being learned. ~ The spiritual picture is taking shape, and some become truly beautiful when the experiences of life are well learned. ~ We want to help you create the most beautiful picture that is possible, to take with you when you return home to Spirit."

Verse 89

Themes:

- Unconditional Love

"We often refer to love. ~ Those of the Earth Plane do not begin to understand the importance of love. ~ First of all, each one must realise that the glorious Being you name as God, is the very essence of love itself. ~ Everything that is of the Earth Plane was created by God out of Himself; in other words everything started as an expression of love. ~ The fact that incarnate souls distort this love does not alter the fact that all is from love. ~ The 'love' that is spoken of by those of the Earth Plane is not love, even as we understand it. ~ At its best it is but a poor imitation of it and it would be better if it was given another name. ~ Most of the time it is lust, which never could be love. ~ We speak of unconditioned love; which is love that will endure forever. ~ Those who have the capacity to understand this quality of unconditioned love have a very great gift. ~ We pray for a time when all of the Earth Plane will – at last – realise that fighting wins nothing of value; when harsh words can never earn the smile of a friend, and when the placing of the burden of guilt on the shoulders of many, is a burden too great for them to carry. ~ When people 'fall in love' it is not true love but an emotion of the moment. It may well last for while but hopefully will grow into something more precious; more akin to the love we in Spirit only begin to understand. ~ That type of love will stand the test of time and can never be lost. ~ Its nature is to expand and to grow throughout eternity. ~ We want you to understand the importance of love and we will refer to it often. ~ It is 'the' one lesson that every soul will have to learn on the journey through eternity; that love *does* indeed conquer all pain, all sadness, in fact all that prevents the Spirit from soaring to the heights. ~ Have love in your heart for all you meet. ~ Those who have the gift of true love will always find friends and happiness wherever they go."

Verse 90

Themes:

- Fear
- Redundancy
- Your unique talent

"Almost everyone on the Earth Plane is inwardly fearful. ~ You may deny this and state that you are not afraid of anything but wait. ~ You may have come to terms with the surface fears; the ones that are obvious, but what about the fears which are deep within your being? ~ Those who hear or read these words know that there is no death – which was a source of fear in past times – you know that it is but a time to move into the next room, and for a while to close the door. ~ It should never be feared, but seen as a promotion to a higher class in the School of Life. ~ Another fear is the loss of a job that would cause hardship to those who are dependent on it to sustain their needs. ~ Many are afraid to launch themselves into an occupation that would bring them more enjoyment and allow expression for their talents and themselves to the full, but are afraid to make that change in the event that it should fail. ~ Life on your Earth should not only be for learning about who you are and where your have come from, but also to express your talents for the benefit of all. ~ It was intended that you should not only enjoy your work but use it to enhance the lives of others. ~ Each one has a specific gift that should be expressed during their lifetime; but often it is the unwillingness to discover the gift, but also to overcome all difficulties, to find the work to express it. ~ That is the true source of satisfaction without first thinking of the money that it may attract. ~ You may ask how you can find out what it is that you should be doing – daily meditation is the obvious answer. ❧ Free yourself from fear and attach yourself to the stream of life and flow with it. ❧ Serving others through your talents will bring joy not only to you but to those you serve. ❧ Everyone can excel in a particular thing, so meditate and ask for Spirit's help to use it; then step forward with confidence and without fear. ❧ Fear will hold you back, but until you try, you will never know the happiness that is just around the corner."

Verse 91

Themes:

- Karma
- Kind thoughts
- Unkind thoughts

"When the time comes to leave the School of Earth, you will be advised to watch your life review*. ❧ As we have said before, for some this can be a painful experience; for you will see in every detail your thoughts, words and deeds. ❧ It *is* painful because you will also see how your thoughts and actions affected other people and the sadness it caused. ❧ It is not compulsory to witness your life review but no progress can be made until this is undertaken. ❧ The reason for this is simple; how can you progress until you are aware of the harm you may have inflicted on others, and be willing to repay each thoughtless act with one of kindness? ❧ When every debt has been repaid then your advisers will help you on your path of progress. ❧ The need to rise higher in understanding of Spirit is inherent in every soul. ❧ There are those who believe that now they are in Heaven – as this is where they think they have arrived – all debts have been forgiven, so why speak of retribution? ❧ It is very hard to convince them that Heaven or not, all past wrong deeds and thinking have to be accounted for. ❧ We say, why wait until your life review before replacing

* The place in which the review takes place is often referred to as the Hall of Mirrors.

every wrong with a right while you are still on the Earth Plane? ❧ Most people know within themselves, where they have done things that they regretted later or said words in the heat of the moment they wish they had not said. ❧ Most will be aware of 'less than kind thoughts' about others but did not think that it mattered, because no-one else knew. ❧ Thoughts are energy, and when 'thought' about another, especially if unkind, go straight to that person and could adversely affect their next action. ❧ All on the Earth Plane live within energy fields and can generate very strong energy fields, especially if they are negative. ❧ Every action and every thought is the transmission of energy to an object or person. ❧ We want you to be aware of all you do and think and be kindly and positive in everything. ❧ In your meditations, recall all you wish you had *not* thought, or said or done and give a kindness in its place. ❧ You do not need to say anything about it, but give someone a pleasant surprise; while in your heart *know* you are repaying a debt you owe to another."

Verse 92

Themes:

- Meditation
- Stillness of the Mind
- The Inner Self

"Be still. ❧ So few in the world at present can be still. ❧ That is not only sitting still, but to still the mind while the body is relaxed. ❧ We do not ask you to acquire a blank mind for that would not be helpful and would be very difficult. ❧ We ask that you slow down your racing thoughts, and begin to still the mind. ❧ While thoughts will come and go, do not catch each one and think about it, just allow it to pass on its way. ❧ When you can do this and with a little practice you will, you will then be able to begin to know who you *really* are. ❧ In the course of this knowing, you will also discover where you come from. ❧ We know you will say that you come from Spirit, but there is more to it than that and with a still mind you will be able to answer that question. ~ There is a whole way of new thinking to discover when you pose these questions. ~ In the answer to these questions – which have puzzled men for many a year – you will find that the whole of your life will have taken on a new understanding. ~ Those things which you thought were closed to you, will now beckon. ~ It will be as if you have been given a new lease of a life where everything is possible. ~ All problems will have their answers within them if you but look deeply. ~ You will find a capacity for love that was denied to you before and there will be a longing to give that love far and wide. ~ It will be an understanding of 'unconditioned love' of which we have often referred, and which many find hard to understand. ~ So much can be realised from the daily practice of being still and meditating. ~ The subject that is used while in meditation is for personal choice, but it is the relaxation of the body and the stilling of the mind which is so important and which we urge you to start to practice. ~ We will add here that you may not reach the point that we have described immediately, but as with all things, patience and determination will win the prize. ~ Ask for your Guides and Helpers to assist you in finding your 'inner self' and all will be well."

Verse 93

Themes:

Conscience · Giving · Natural Laws

"In every field of human activity and endeavour, the inner desire is to be a success. ~ There is no-one who embarks upon a career who thinks they will be a failure. ~ The young person, who has attained adulthood, sees themselves as shining in their efforts, and in so doing will make a difference in the world for the good of others. ~ The inner desire is to fulfil a deep longing for making the world a better place when they leave it, than when they first arrived. ~ That desire is placed in the heart of all souls in order to advance the Plan of Creation which was put into progress at the Beginning. ❧ It is not enough to have this desire for itself and hope that fate or destiny will do the rest. ❧ It takes vision, effort, as well as determination to carry it through as most have discovered. There is one sure way to place your feet on the road to success and that is to give yourself to the task in hand. ❧ Whatever is to be done in the course of your work, give freely of yourself in the work itself, even if you dislike that part of the work. Remember that whatever effort you put in, you will get out. ❧ It applies to those you work with too. ❧ If you work well with others and are well disposed towards them, they will repay you with their friendship and help in a moment of need. ❧ Kindness in all its forms never goes unrewarded. ❧ We do not suggest that you should plan your efforts to obtain the maximum reward; this Law of sowing and reaping does not perform quite like that. ❧ It is the attitude of mind – without the consideration of any return – that brings benefit. ❧ It comes under the Natural Laws of the Universe. ❧ These Laws cannot be exploited by humanity. ❧ Cause and effect wins the day in every case; they cannot be manipulated to please the wiles of man. ❧ They are God's Laws and cannot be broken without penalty. ❧ These Natural Laws are known deep within each soul; they are the knowledge of right from wrong, and known as conscience."

Verse 94

Themes:
Ignorance   Spiritual Knowledge

"Knowledge is power. ❧ These words have often been said by those in your world who have understanding of what it really means. ❧ At the same time, there are others who have said that ignorance is bliss. ❧ For anyone to perpetrate ignorance is the worst thing that can happen. ❧ There is no doubt that the ignorant suffer because they can be manipulated and exploited, being led this way and that and not knowing what is happening to them. ❧ In times past, the priests kept their flocks in ignorance of the nature of Spirit, because they may be asked questions that they either would not know the answer to, or because it was not good for their people to know. ❧ It was a time when few were able to read and had to rely on what the priests told them. ❧ In this way the priests were able to control their flocks by perpetrating their ignorance. ❧ If questions were asked, they were told to have faith. ❧ That was no help to a mother grieving for a child she thought she had lost, or for anyone dearly loved who had died. ❧ Those priests were not able to give any reassurance of the continuation of life on another plane of existence. ❧ A glimmer of light began to penetrate your world, which brought hope to many. ❧ The knowledge of Spirit was brought to the Earth Plane. ❧ In past times there were those who knew of Spirit and spoke of their knowledge, but the power of the priests soon got rid of them; for if allowed to continue would destroy the power of the Church. ❧ Now this knowledge has got a firm foothold it will grow, but be wary, there are still those who would crush it if at all possible. ❧ In your material world *too* much knowledge can be dangerous for some, but Spiritual knowledge is like a breath of fresh air to a drowning man. ❧ It can also be likened to an armoury; with it you can protect yourself and others and bring the balm of healing to all who need it. ❧ It will bring strength and courage in times of hardship and enable each one to search out the reason for *their* life on the Earth Plane. ❧ Above all it encourages times to be quiet, to listen and understand the voice of God within."

Verse 95

Themes:
'Dark' Communities   Spiritual Light

"We have often said that when we draw close to the Plane of Earth, we are immediately aware of how dark, damp and cold it is. ❧ This is something we accept and easily overcome because we want to come and offer our help and guidance where we are welcome. ❧ Even on a warm summer's day, your world is still a dark place. ❧ You see the brilliance of the sunshine and assume that is the light of which we speak, but it is not. ❧ The light of the Sun is of a material nature to directly benefit the Earth. ❧ We speak of spiritual light, which gives light to our world. ❧ It is not only streaming from the Highest Realms, but those who live here give out their light by their very presence. ❧ There are some planes where the light is quite dim, and it is because little spiritual light is given out. We have referred to the dark areas where there is no light at all, because its inhabitants have turned from the light completely and therefore give nothing. ❧ Many of us volunteer to work in such areas in an attempt to rescue those souls from themselves, but it is a distressing experience and can be tolerated for short periods only. ❧ Where God's light cannot penetrate, it is true hardship for any who work there. ❧ It would be similar for you to be starved of food; you would begin to feel your strength failing and so it is with us in those dark areas. ❧ We do have successes and these spur us on to go on trying. ❧ When there is a change in one who has resided in darkness for a very long time, their appearance – which was hideous – begins to change, and a faint glow is discernable around them. ❧ It is then that we know that they are listening to us and are prepared to give our words a chance. ❧ Those who give out much light and understand the ways of Spirit find that *their* light becomes brighter, and with the increase in their light, they are drawn like a magnet toward the fountain of all that is Light and Love. ~ The material world is a means to know and aspire to the inner longings of the Spirit."

Verse 96

Themes:

- Evolution
- Light Workers
- Plan of Creation
- Rebellion

"When young people leave childhood behind and are about to claim their majority, there is often a sense of rebellion against the ideas of their parents, and this makes itself known in expressions of bad behaviour. ~ The adults cannot understand this behaviour and speak harshly to their offspring. Now look at the wider scene; in fact look across your world and you will see similar behaviour. ~ Peoples are aware that former ways must be left behind because they are being outgrown. ~ It is inevitable that there will be rebellion because, on the one hand they do not want to be told what to do, and on the other the future looks uncertain and menacing. For all their rebellion, coupled with the feeling that they know best – often the hallmark of approaching maturity – they know that whatever they do or say cannot stop them reaching that point – which is what they fear! ~ Evolution and progress is inevitable and there will be many changes within the Earth itself, as well as its people, and this is what is causing this turmoil. ~ You will begin to notice that many of the children now coming to the Earth Plane seem to have knowledge of a special task ahead of them. ~ We do not mean that *you* do not have such a task, because everyone is special in the eyes of the Creator. ~ We mean that the new generation is *aware* of this special task and they come to you with special knowledge which will be instrumental in smoothing the way for the new ideas which are to follow. ~ There are many now in our world that are being given this knowledge which will help them guide the less able already on the Earth Plane. ~ We want you to see all the troubles on the Earth as 'prolonged growing pains' that will lead eventually to a kinder and more peaceful Earth Plane. ~ The changeover will take many years of your time. ~ But your work is to continue to spread the word that there is no death, but an active World of Spirit to help the peoples of the Earth to forge a better world for all God's creation."

Verse 97

Themes:

- Differences
- Knowledge
- Media news coverage

"At one time when the Earth was younger, an event in one part of your world took many days, weeks or even longer for the knowledge of it to become known to other parts of the Earth Plane. ~ Now, with the advances in your technology, events can be known as they occur. ~ It may seem to most an advantage but we would question that idea? ~ Much of what is shown in an instance of your time, is of violence happening or instances of horror. ~ We think this has an unfortunate effect on the minds of many people. ~ Ignorance or misunderstanding of these happenings brings fear of the people concerned with it, and suspicion of foreigners is the result. ~ At one time those of another country were to be welcomed because of their novelty value. ~ Then, when they were better known, it was found that they were able to contribute to the well-being of the community they found themselves within. ~ When you meet those of another culture and begin to understand them, it is obvious that people are all the same in reality, but lack of knowledge and ignorance of their way of life breeds mistrust and fear. ~ Deep down, those of Earth are all the same but at *different* levels of understanding. All were created from the Godhead from Love itself. ~ The different skin colour is to protect the individual from the effect of the sun. ~ That in itself should not be a reason to look upon them as unworthy. ❧ They are as much a part of the great plan of Creation as are you. ❧ There is no-one superior or inferior. ❧ There is no-one to judge such matters. ❧ Regardless of nationality, each one incarnates for the purpose of learning the necessary lessons to progress along the road to perfection. ❧ It is true that some are more advanced spiritually than others, but all are on the Earth Plane to learn. ❧ Even those less advanced can teach valuable lessons to the more spiritually advanced. ❧ It is for this reason that no-one should judge, hate or harm another that God has created. ❧ Use your technology to learn of the culture of those you mistrust, and come to know them as your friends."

Verse 98

Themes:

- Earth Changes
- Light Workers
- Spiritual Rebirth
- The Spiritual Movement

"We have warned you for some time now, that you should be prepared for the many changes that are to take place within the Earth Plane. ❧ Some of you may look upon the Earth as a huge rocky lump that remains the same throughout the centuries, but this is not so. ❧ It is changing all the time, if only in modest ways. ❧ The Earth Plane is a living being, but because it does not have a physical body in the accepted human sense, many cannot understand it as living and breathing. ❧ Its cycle of life is vastly different from your own but because it lives, so you can live. ❧ There are many large lumps of rocks in the universes that cannot support life because they do not live. ❧ The many universes, which you see as points of light in the night sky, are all part of the Plan of Creation. ❧ Life cannot stand still. ❧ Each day *you* are changing and so is all that has been created by God for His purpose. ❧ These changes that are to come will be the result of the Earth breathing out as it were, before taking another breath. ❧ The

Earth has taken many shallow breaths before but this is to be a deep breath. ❧ The space between the breaths is not calculable in Earth time, but it has happened before as your scientists can tell you. ❧ Those of you who *do* understand about the World of Spirit must be prepared to help each other when this time of need occurs. ❧ There will be some confusion, because of a lack of understanding of what is happening, but it will be to those who can offer comfort and healing who will be in demand. ❧ Strength and inspiration will be given to you to help and many will be brought into an understanding of Spirit. ❧ You will act as ambassadors for us, bringing a ray of hope and calm when all seems lost. ❧ Those who undertake to help will receive protection. ❧ Many wonders will be seen and the veil between Earth and Spirit will appear very thin indeed. ❧ Do not fear for you will be guided."

This reading was given on 9th May 1999.

Verse 99

Themes:

- Life in Spirit
- Spiritual Progress
- The Purpose of Life

"When you were created, you began your journey out of pure light and pure love. ❧ God is pure love and because of that love there shines a pure light. ❧ You were not aware of yourself at that time as the gift of consciousness was not yet bestowed upon you. ❧ Many processes – for want of a better term – had to be undergone before you were clothed ready for your journey to the Earth Plane. ❧ Pure Spirit cannot live on the Plane of Earth. ❧ Your body that you inhabit while on the Earth Plane is constructed of the matter of the Earth Plane and has to be left behind when you are called back to the World of Spirit. ❧ When you leave your Earth body in death, you will discover that you have another that is exactly the same and is the body you will use while in the World of Spirit. ꩜ As you learn and progress, you may notice that your body will become finer. ꩜ This may not be apparent to the individual but can be noticed by the change in the colour, and the pattern on the hem of the garment that you wear. ꩜ On the journey through the many planes of progress you will leave behind yet another of the many bodies that you have. ꩜ There are many more bodies, each finer than the last. ꩜ It could be likened to another death, which is another word for the shedding of an unwanted body. ꩜ In the course of eternity and consistent progress and understanding, all the protective bodies will be shed and will reveal the completed Spirit now clothed in light alone. ꩜ That is the wondrous moment when your journey to perfection will be ended. ꩜ However, we are told that although that is the ultimate goal there will never be an end to progress. ꩜ To become part of the Godhead is too wonderful an aspiration to speak about. ꩜ We cannot tell you about it because there are no words available for its description, and we must add here that we have a long way to go before being able to even glimpse such glory. ꩜ We do know that the path towards it is both joy and happiness."

Verse 100

Themes:

- Angels
- Free Will
- Respecting Nature
- Summer

"Your summer is upon you and most of you will enjoy this time by going into your gardens or open spaces and be aware of the natural order of things. ꩜ Spend time to notice the insects, bees and birds going about their own little lives. ꩜ Remember they do not have free choice, as do you. ꩜ They are compelled to do what they do by the will of the Supreme Being. ꩜ They are provided with all they need and the means by which to get it. ꩜ They do not complain because such a thought could not be theirs. ~ It is at such times of thinking that we wonder why it was that the Supreme Being decided that humanity alone should be given this gift. ~ The Angelic Beings were not asked to find perfection through experience and therefore were not given the gift of free choice. ~ They are perfect and know they are perfect, but do help their lesser brethren through compassion. ~ There have been many reports by those of Earth that an Angelic Being helped at a moment of need and then apparently faded from sight. ~ Usually such reports are dismissed with the idea that the recipient had a vivid imagination. ~ Angelic Beings do visit the Earth Plane to assist their brethren towards the goal – which is already theirs – as they are part of the Godhead. ~ Their work is in keeping the order of the Universe. ~ If Earth beings were allowed to do everything that they would wish to do, chaos would follow immediately. ~ We say you have 'free choice' but there has to be some restriction or the Earth would have been destroyed by now. ~ The Angelic Beings will not allow this to happen but you have sufficient freedom for *all* your needs. ~ That is why we urge you to go into open spaces to see Nature at work, and marvel at the way each creature depends on every other creature and plant for its survival. ~ It is time to understand Nature and to work with it if you seek a fulfilled, abundant life. ~ The Supreme Being has lavished His love on the Plane of Earth and its people, but the time has long passed when there must be a response of understanding."

This reading was given on 13th June 1999.

Verse 101

Themes:
- Ambitions
- Future
- Life Plan
- The Unknown

"Most people like to feel that they are in control of their lives. To have no purpose and aimlessly wander from job to job would be considered irresponsible. ❧ Most have families to consider and there are few who would not want the best for their children. ❧ That is why everyone has an aim whether it is possible to realise it or not. ❧ Aim high and keep that goal in the forefront of all thinking when it comes to planning for the future. ❧ However, while making these plans, there should also be an awareness of the unknown. ❧ Allowance must always be made for the event that slips into the situation and immediately changes all the well-laid plans. ❧ To many it comes as a shock and for a while there is confusion as to what should be done next. ❧ Those who meditate are aware that the element of the unknown is ever present and do not feel confused or frustrated if that event comes into *their* picture. ❧ Fighting this intrusion is of little use and the only course is to accept the new situation with good grace. ❧ New plans must be made, but this time it is wise to include the possibility that the unknown element may again show itself. ❧ There is another way of looking at this uninvited unknown. ❧ If it is examined carefully it may be bringing a message to the planner. ❧ Perhaps the wrong course of action is to be taken and the World of Spirit is attempting to prevent a mistake being made. ❧ Remember, we cannot directly influence those we wish to inspire but it is possible for us to make the individual think again about an imminent course of action. ❧ The unknown is always a large part of the life of each one, but do not fear. ❧ The well-worn path is not for everyone and those who want to progress must be prepared to take a step on a path that may be without signposts! ❧ Fear inhibits all progress. ❧ Those who place their faith in Spirit – and with daily meditation – will find the future a wonderful experience. ❧ Ask for courage each day and we will be there to guide and inspire you."

Verse 102

Themes:

Forgiveness   Unconditional Love

"We have spoken to you before about forgiveness, but we wish to bring it to your attention again. ~ In the rush and clamour of life in your world today, it becomes even more important to think about forgiveness. ~ Events take place at such an alarming rate for you that often you have some difficulty, because there is no time in which to reflect and take stock. ~ We want you to take that necessary time, not only for reflection, but to forgive yourself. ~ Just as you must love yourself so you must learn to forgive yourself. ~ If you let it pass by, you will find it will build up in the background and cause you heartache later on in your life. ~ The next course is to forgive others. We know that is often the hardest part of life, especially if another has done a serious wrong to you. ~ It is then that the last advice you want to hear is to forgive that person. ~ Look at it in different way. ~ Whatever is done cannot be undone, but to think ill will toward that person will not help them to change, but most importantly, it will hold up *your* spiritual progress. ~ It may not seem relevant to link forgiveness with spiritual progress but you will find it so. ~ True unconditioned love for others will allow you to forgive another whatever they have done. ~ It is a hard lesson, but is so worthwhile to take it into meditation and find the answer for yourself. ~ Ask for help in this understanding. ~ It may take some time to come to a true understanding of unconditional love. ~ When you do understand, you will be able to forgive those who hurt you, knowing that it is because they do not understand the Law of Love. ~ You will come through this personal experience with a different outlook on life in general, and be determined not to hurt others, but to bring tolerance into *all* your activities. ~ In your meditations you will find the answers you seek, if you ask for help from the Planes of Spirit and God's Blessing on all your endeavours."

Verse 103

Themes:
Colour Creed Race

"Many times we have said that each of you was created and individualised from the Godhead out of Love. ~ You were created perfect, because God is perfect and knows nothing of the effect of the human turning away from the perfection of God. ~ When you became an individual Spirit you were not of any particular race, nor were you coloured, nor did you hold to a particular culture. ~ All these things belong to the Earth incarnation. ~ In themselves, they do not infer that one way of life is any better than another, nor does it mean that one colour should be dominant over another. ~ The reason for an incarnation of one Spirit to be in Africa is for the experience it will offer that individual. ~ This does not mean that each incarnation must always be in Africa. ~ At this point, you will also understand that the reason for colour difference is the Earth climate in the region of that incarnation, and of course, the effect that the parents will have on the incoming Spirit. ~ Now you will say that if the individualised Spirit starts perfect, then why is it necessary to have to visit Earth at all? ~ The perfect Spirit does not know it is perfect for it has nothing with which to compare, but the 'knowing' will always be there. ~ In order to be able to be a valuable worker in the Plan of Creation, all possible experiences of human life are needed to enable each one to offer the highest and best, backed up by knowledge and understanding. ~ With all that experience, the journey towards perfection is one of joy and excitement. ~ Because of your original state of perfection you know through all your difficulties that you are on your way home. ~ It therefore does not matter what colour, creed or race the individual proclaims, it is what has been learned and understood; and whether love in all its meanings formed the rock of each incarnation. ~ We urge you therefore not to think that one colour or culture is above another; it is what each one can offer others on the path towards home and the Creator of all that is."

Verse 104

Themes:
- Incarnate Soul
- Who am I?

"Have you ever wondered who you really are? ∾ We are sure that it would have passed through your mind at some time, but because an answer was not forthcoming the question was dismissed. ∾ It may be many years before you will find the answer. ∾ You all know that you were created out of Love itself but that does not tell you who you are. ∾ As soon as you take your first breath on Earth you are given a label, a name. ∾ Then, from that day onwards you are known by that name. ∾ If you do not like that name you can change it, but *you* will have chosen another name, another label. ∾ Everything has a label for reasons of identification, but it is only a label and does not inform as to the nature or quality of the thing. ∾ During your life on the Earth Plane you will play many different roles. ∾ You begin by being a son or a daughter, and at the same time you could be a brother or a sister to another child. ∾ While you are so young, the centre of your life will be your Mother, and it will be only later that you will become aware that your Mother is also a wife, who will play other roles apart from her attending to *your* needs. ∾ Even though you are now aware of all these things, you still have not discovered who you really are. ∾ By now you will have found that you are more than just your body, and that by going 'within' to the still and sacred place that you will find out who you are. ∾ It may take many lives and many questions but you will find the answer. ∾ Your inner being is vast and for many a long time you may hesitate on the threshold, but the need for knowing will give you the courage to enter and be embraced by the One who is far greater than you could ever be, for all your experiences. ∾ At last – through knowledge – you will have come home never to feel abandoned ever again. ◌ That 'inner knowing' surpasses all that has ever gone before and with it the realisation that the journey was worth all the suffering and the unknowing."

Verse 105

Themes:

- Choice
- Impatience
- Perfect Career
- Spirit Guides

"We have spoken before about choice. ◌ Each one makes choices every day in the course of living, and does not realise that a choice is being made. ◌ There are choices, which must be made which *do* have great significance in the life of each one. ◌ The time comes when the road ahead seems to fork or it may even appear to be crossroads, and the question is then, which one is the right one? ◌ When faced with this problem it is wise to sit quietly and ask the question of your 'inner self'. ◌ You may not get the answer immediately but wait a little and have patience. ◌ Impatience almost always makes the wrong choice. ◌ If you have trust in the wisdom of the One Supreme Being then you will get the answer. ◌ Those who are always with you have your happiness and well-being at heart, and will try to impress you with the choice to be made. ◌ They cannot tell you what to do, but will give you the feeling of each possibility. ◌ Think deeply about all that comes to mind when in the silence and you will guided in the right direction. ◌ Anything that may change the course of your life should receive due consideration. ◌ Remember too that the way which seems attractive from the outside, may not be quite what you had hoped for when you are committed to it. That is why we urge you to go into the silence and ask for guidance. ◌ When the choice is for a new job, it is not always the one that offers the most that is the right one. ◌ Each should be happy in their chosen work of life. ◌ In much of your world the pressure for more money and power only brings greater stress and strain, and the 'more' of everything cannot be enjoyed because of the suffering that its achievement has brought. ~ Whatever the choice, consideration should be given as to how it will affect others and the long-term personal effects. ~ A snap decision without asking for help may lead to sorrows and experiences that were unnecessary. ~ Go forward with the help of Spirit and find a life of fulfilment."

Verse 106

Themes:
Emotions · Feeling · Healing · Senses

"On arrival on the Earth Plane, each one is equipped with the basic senses of sight, touch, hearing, smell and taste. ~ These are provided in order to find the way around and to discover food, which will sustain the body. ~ There is an additional sense which makes life worthwhile: it is that of feeling. Without a sense of feeling there would have been no artists, musicians or anyone with a creative flair for making life more beautiful. ~ It is this need for beauty – in all its forms – that distinguishes the human from the animal. ~ This sense of feeling extends into other areas of human life. ~ In order to live successfully with others there is a need to be aware of the feelings of others. ~ One cannot consider feelings without thinking of love. ~ Love can evoke the deepest of human feelings as can the apparent loss of love – as in bereavement. ~ These are very deep human emotions and those who understand them are able to communicate with others and help them in their hour of need. ~ To reach an understanding it must be possible to touch the Spirit. ~ It is in this activity that a true healing can be achieved. ~ When you see another in trouble or who is grieving for a loved one, there is no help on the 'superficial level' that can reach them. ~ Through understanding human emotions, you can help with words of comfort that can touch the Spirit and a healing will take place. ~ It may not be at that moment but to give those words of comfort will enable the grieving one to draw help from Spirit, and begin to understand their own depth of feeling. ~ It is through deep involvement of one's own emotions and feeling that each one can help the other. ~ Once you have plumbed the depths of sadness, rejection or whatever the cause of despair, then it is the understanding of it that can be of help to others. ~ It is this gift of feeling that enables each one to taste the beauty and joy of life and to appreciate the depth of human love and understanding. ~ We want you to remember that when in need, your Spirit Helpers are always there to offer strength and support if only you will ask."

Verse 107

Themes:
Conscience · Evil · Tolerance

"Almost every day on the Earth Plane there are events taking place that many class as being evil. ~ Here we want you to think about what evil is. ~ It would seem an easy answer but it is not. ~ What is evil or wrong to one is not evil or wrong to another. ~ We agree that the taking of a life is very wrong but one should go further than just condemnation. ~ There are large numbers of people who do not have a strong distinction between right and wrong. ~ Perhaps they have had no instruction as to the existence of a Supreme Being in whatever belief is followed by the community. ~ If the individual does not accept there is a Supreme Being, it cannot be assumed that the members of that community know right from wrong, and that the taking of a life is wrong. ~ There are some peoples who believe that it is right to kill your prisoners rather than rehabilitate them. ~ It is not only the taking of life but it applies to many other aspects of human living. ~ You have all been placed in the great melting pot of life to learn to live together and to try to understand each other and learn the skill of being tolerant. ~ In any way that it applies, evil or sin is the turning away from the Glorious One who created you. ~ He gave you the most precious gift of free will. ~ If you exercise this gift by doing just as you like, without giving consideration to the effect it will have on others, then you have turned away from the Will of *your* Creator. ~ To help you in the difficulties that confront everyone on the Earth Plane, the Supreme Being has given you a conscience, to offer guidance during those difficult periods when you know not where to turn. ~ That conscience is the spark of your Creator within your being. ~ Every human on the Earth has this conscience to guide them. ~ If that small voice is ignored, then in time it will not be heard – but it is *always* there. ~ There is no excuse for any person to say they did not know. ~ Whatever is the wrong that is done, there will have to be a time of repayment. ~ This can be most painful when all the wrongs are put together for recompense."

Verse 108

Themes:
Abilities · Appearance · Self Worth

"Be happy with the way you appear to others as well as yourself. Accept the way you are in your manner, not reluctantly nor with blind acceptance, but with joy. ~ You are what you are! ~ Have confidence in the 'you' you see in the mirror, and do not bemoan your lot in your appearance. ~ By so doing, you are questioning the way the Father of all wanted you to be. ~ You are a means to an answer for many others. ~ You may have a defect that is obvious to others, or you may feel you are not as handsome or as beautiful as others that you see each day. Those things are of no consequence and should be ignored. Some will spend much of their resources on attempting to change what was given to them. ~ Even when all is to your liking, are you any better off? ~ You may feel you are in some way improved but real improvement comes from within. Concentrate your thinking time with having kindly thoughts about others and be willing to help those who are in some way disfigured to value themselves. ~ Each one has much to contribute if only the emphasis is not placed on how the individual looks. ~ Looks alone can do nothing. ~ It may help to lift your self esteem but looks change with the fashion of times. ~ A greater service can be rendered to another by getting them to understand that they are loved and valued for the way they are, not for the way they might be if their nose was straighter or their chin was less prominent. ~ Be thankful for the way you are, and make the most of the abilities that you have. ~ Look after your body, for it is your 'house' until you are called home to Spirit. ~ Ensure too, just as you care for the body, that you also care for the 'inner you' keeping that as clean and as pure as is possible on the Earth Plane. ~ Keep your mind ever open to the inspirations of the World of Spirit and lead others into knowledge and understanding. ~ Remain peaceful and calm, knowing that whatever life presents to you, you are able, with the aid of your Helpers, to take full advantage of every event and learn from them whatever is required for progress."

Verse 109

Themes:

- Atheists
- Devious People
- Understanding People

"Clothing serves many purposes. ~ It keeps the physical body warm if you live in a cool or cold climate. ~ Even in a hot climate, a small amount of covering is considered necessary for the sake of privacy. ~ In these Earth days, clothing is used to show off new ideas in style and colours. ~ For us in the World of Spirit, clothing serves an entirely different purpose. ~ From the garment that is worn, we see from the pattern how much understanding you have of spiritual matters. ➰ This is very important to us, because we then know the level of teaching you need at any time. ➰ Looking at a group of people we can see how we could help with *our* knowledge. ➰ Although we come to offer our help to you to make understanding easier, *we* are learning too. ➰ It is by contact with the Earth Plane that our understanding is also advanced. ➰ It is by this constant interaction that all are helped along the road of progress. ➰ It is unfortunate that you are not able to see from the covering: the real person and *their* true thinking about the matter in hand. On the Earth Plane, it is easy to say one thing to please the listener and at the same time to think quite different thoughts! There is no way for most to know the difference. ➰ It is only by experience of people and their ways that those of Earth learn *not* to trust anyone. ➰ If you are one who has the gift to see the aura of the one you are asked to trust, you will be guided to make the right decision. ➰ Before you make any important decision please ask for inner guidance before you give your answer. ➰ It is those who are devious in earthly matters who really believe that death is the end and they will not be found out about *their* behaviour. ➰ We can tell you that it comes as a great shock when they realise that they are not dead and their misdeeds are there for all to see. ➰ All *you* are is known, and must be accounted for whether good or not so good."

Verse 110

Themes:

Letting go of the Past · Living in the Now

"We can see that much of the unhappiness that surrounds many people is caused by the concern and worry over the past. It is a pointless exercise to carry the baggage of the past around with you wherever you go. ➰ There is one very important point to make and that is this: you cannot change one split second of any of it, no matter how much you worry about it. No matter how many times you go over it and say the famous words: 'If only I had done or not done this, or said or not said those words,' it will get you nowhere and continue to cause much misery and unhappiness. ❧ Whatever has happened in the past, or whatever mistakes were made, it was all experience and teaches each one *not* to allow a similar happening again. It is in this way that each one is enabled to learn. ❧ It was for those reasons that you were given this life in the School of Earth in order to learn these things – which would be difficult to learn once you arrive in the World of Spirit. ❧ We do not advocate spending all thinking time in the future either. There are many whose concern is always tomorrow. ❧ We agree that some consideration should be given to future plans and activities but should be kept to a reasonable interest. What we are leading up to is the eternal NOW. ❧ Much of the misery will be avoided if you will live in the NOW. ❧ To do this you leave the past as a teaching experience. ❧ Tomorrow has not yet arrived and no-one can be absolutely certain that there will be a tomorrow as a member of the Earth Plane. ❧ Therefore all you have is NOW. ❧ Live in the NOW and the weight of the past will drop from your shoulders. ❧ Tomorrow will take care of itself when you live in the NOW. ❧ We accept that it will take a little practice but it is well worth the effort. ❧ There is nothing wrong in recalling past events but not to keep going over them. ❧ Live in the NOW first and be aware of the difference. ❧ Be aware of all that is occurring now and all that is around you in all its God-given beauty."

Verse 111

Themes:

- Life's Lessons
- Negative Thinking
- Positive Thinking

"Everyone wants life to be successful, peaceful and happy, and that is what we would wish it to be for all. ∾ Unfortunately this is often not so. ∾ Instead of happy, positive thoughts, many will indulge in negative thinking. ∾ As you well know, thoughts are things, and the more they are thought the stronger they will become. ∾ It is then that the thing 'most dreaded' happens and without the full understanding of what you have done. ∾ Then of course, you are full of misery, but why? ∾ You have created it! ∾ When your thoughts are about happy things, better things happen to you. ∾ Negative thinking is when you dwell on past events when you know you cannot change any of it. ∾ Also any thoughts of envy or jealousy of another's achievements; these thoughts destroy the individual from the inside. ∾ Such thoughts eat into the inner-being and if persisted in will attract disease to the body. Whatever your situation at the moment; however strained or difficult to control; don't fight against it. ∾ Do all you can to sort out the situation, but once you have done all you can, leave it and just accept it with as good grace as you can. ∾ Set it aside and do not dwell upon it and you will find that it will change quite gradually and you will see your way through. ∾ Often the secret in a difficult situation is acceptance. ∾ We know that it is difficult to do but be reassured that if you can, you will win the day. ∾ Some people have very hard problems to overcome, but the lesson is in the way that problem is handled. ∾ Try the acceptance method first, instead of wearing yourself out by fighting. ∾ Therefore we say keep calm, keep positive and accept without recriminations. ∾ We agree that it is not easy, but if it *was* then there would be no point in the lessons and you would learn nothing. ∾ When these blocks and rough patches are strewn across your pathway; you will usually find that there is a lesson to be found within. Ask for God's strength and courage each day to help you through these hard times."

Verse 112

Themes:
 Happiness Living in the NOW Nature

"Most people are searching for something or even perhaps someone. ~ Sometimes the search is realised but more often than not there is a sense of frustration. ~ Inner questions are asked as to why it is they cannot achieve their goal. ~ All they ask for is perhaps more money, so that they can have 'the thing' that would bring them happiness? ~ It may bring pleasure for a while, but happiness we do not think so. ~ Any material attainment will bring pleasure but it cannot bring happiness. The material world is only an allusion; if it were not so, then the attainment of goods would bring more than just a passing pleasure. ~ The apparent needs of yesterday are forgotten today because they were just passing pleasures. ~ Everybody on the Plane of Earth is seeking happiness, but the truth of happiness has been missed by most, because they have been looking in the wrong place. ~ As we have said before, happiness comes from within. ~ Wealth and possessions can be a burden and be the cause of great unhappiness; likewise poverty causes untold unhappiness mainly because of the lack of the essential needs of life. ~ Acceptance of your current position is the key to finding happiness. ~ Whatever your situation, we advise that you should accept it for what it is. Before you begin to think about it remember that there is always someone else who has less than you have. ~ In your mind think about 'the thing' that you thought would bring that elusive happiness. ~ Then, accept that for the time being you cannot have it, and you will accept and make do with what you *do* have. ~ Fill your thoughts with all that is around you; the trees bursting their buds, the flowers lifting their faces to the sun and the birds welcoming the new day. ~ These things you can appreciate and thank God that they are there to see. ~ True happiness is understanding that those things that are God-given do not change; they are not passing illusions; even the rich man can lose everything! ~ We want you to thank God each day for all the Blessings that you have and to unfold that 'inner happiness' to enrich your life."

Verse 113

Themes:
- Incarnation
- The Purpose of Life

"Incarnation into the World of Matter is not accidental. ~ You agreed to a life on the Earth Plane for a purpose, and it is for *you* to discover that purpose. ~ You cannot expect someone else to find it for you. ~ Those who have asked themselves that question and found the answer, usually find life fulfilling. ~ You bring with you a talent or gift, sometimes more than one. ~ This gift is unique to you in that no-one else can express it in the same way as you can. ~ It is the expression that provides that special quality. ~ When you have discovered *your* gift it will need to be trained in order for it to reach its best quality. ~ Many will have achieved this by the time they are adult but it is never too late to discover your talent. ~ It is what you do with your ability that is most important. ~ If you only think about making as much money as possible without regard to others, you may well do so but you will not be happy. ~ Bringing all you have to offer in the service to others is the key to happiness in life on the Earth Plane. ~ Remember, *your* special talent was given as a gift, and though it needed training, it is still a gift and should be used for the benefit of others first and foremost. ~ Whatever you are good at doing may be your gift. ~ It is in the giving of service – using your gift – that you will bring pleasure to you and others and *that* is the beginning of experiencing a happy life. ❧ If you have not found *your* purpose and talent ask your Helpers the question when in meditation. ❧ Books cannot supply the answers to those sorts of questions. ❧ Meditate every day if only for a few minutes. ❧ You will find this contact with your inner being brings a feeling of peace. ❧ We will state again that you, a unique spiritual being, came to the Plane of Earth for a purpose in the Plan of Creation. ❧ You came with a talent to express for the benefit of others, and it is up to each one to discover that talent and purpose for a happy and fulfilling life."

Verse 114

Themes:
- Earth Changes
- Human Behaviour

"Many will have realised that the promised changes to the Earth Plane are already taking place. ❧ Those who live on the Earth bring some of these changes about, but others are the result of the speeding up of the vibrations of the planet. ❧ We often hear said that time seems to pass more quickly now than ever before. ❧ Some of you may have thought – when we first spoke of these changes – that all would happen in a matter of months causing instant chaos, but this could never be. ❧ There will be sudden events that will cause much upheaval and disruption to daily life but these changes are necessary and were laid down many moons ago. ❧ As we have said, some of it has occurred ahead of its time by human action but would have happened anyway at some time. ❧ Whether you have heard about these changes or not, there is an inner awareness that something is afoot. ❧ This feeling has caused a restlessness that makes itself known in many different ways. Young people are said to be out of control, and going about causing people to fear for their safety. ❧ There seems to be *any* excuse to cause mayhem and general disruption to the way of life of others. ~ Young children are no longer able to be free to play out in the fresh air, without some sort of supervision, in case they are molested by those who should know better. ~ This is all a type of rebellion at the inner knowledge of these changes. ~ Those that act in this way do not want these changes and are trying to resist *any* change. ~ They liked things the way they were. ~ On the surface, they are not aware of it in quite this way, but it is so. ~ We want to assure you that nothing ever stays the same; *all* has to evolve however slow this evolving takes. ~ We want you all to be aware of Spirit and grow in spiritual understanding. ~ With this growth, human behaviour will have to change, for one goes with the other. ~ Cultivate inner peace, in order to face any difficulty that may beset you and ask your loving Father God to bless you and give you courage to face each day."

This reading was given on 21st May 2000.

Verse 115

Themes:
Doctors · Future of Medicine · Healers

"For a great many of your Earth years, your doctors have made a point of studying disease. ~ In this, they have become very knowledgeable and can dispense pills and potions that will treat almost anything that the physical body can have wrong with it – at least that is what is mostly claimed. ~ This may be true up to a point, but all peoples are lumped together under the heading of a particular disease. ~ As we have so often said, each being is an individual; created an individual by the Supreme Being you know as God. ~ This means that each one is unique in that no one's vibration is exactly the same as another. ~ It is for this reason that many treatments seem to go wrong in that the tablets are too strong for *that* particular person or the course of treatment should have been taken more slowly. ☙ There is a time – which is rapidly approaching – when the doctors will realise that they have the whole study the wrong way round. ☙ They will realise that they *should* study health and the harmony of the body. ☙ When they do that, they will begin to understand that each of the organs within the body works towards the harmony of the whole and – though each organ vibrates differently – that each compensates for the others. ☙ From this careful study there will come a different understanding of the physical body and a new partnership with the healing fraternity will begin. ☙ Until now, most doctors look upon the healers as below their consideration, because they do not have their qualifications. ☙ On the surface this may be true but *they* have left out the most important part, in that the input of Spirit has been left out of *their* disease training. ☙ The healer, who is used as an instrument in the healing process, can do as much and sometimes more than the conventional doctor. ☙ When the doctors will agree to work with the healers, then a higher quality of healing will take place. ☙ It is not only on the physical level that we speak but there must be established an understanding that pure thoughts and aims to maintain 'harmony' within the body are necessary. When the doctors understand that harmony must exist in the life around each one that they treat, so will begin an awareness of tolerance towards all."

Verse 116

Themes:
- Incarnation
- Guardian
- Guides
- Helpers
- Soul Groups

"In these short readings, we try to give you some idea of life in our World of Spirit. ☙ We try also to give spiritual application to material and worldly matters. ☙ We are not preaching, but giving encouragement to do your best in difficult circumstances. ☙ Every right thought and right effort brings its own reward at a later time. ❧ All of you belong to a spiritual family group. ❧ There are of course many such groups, but the group you were assigned to when you were individualised remains throughout eternity. ❧ You will realise that the group – every group – is very large. ❧ Not all of any group will incarnate at the same time. ❧ Those of *your* own group you will meet throughout your life, perhaps as friends, family members or even those you only meet from time to time but on first meeting 'feel' that you know them; you seem to have so much in common with them. ❧ This may have happened to you and now you will know the reason. ❧ Those with close friends of long standing will have known each other through many lives. ❧ There may have been a family relationship, but in any case, to be so closely associated is a blessing indeed. ❧ To have found *your* affinity or eternal partner is a *very* special blessing and few are blessed this way. ❧ There is always a golden thread that runs throughout the group, which can never be broken. ❧ Not every member of your group will incarnate together. ❧ Those that remain in our World of Spirit will often act as Helpers or Advisors for those on the physical plane. ❧ There is frequent meeting with those who have not taken a physical body when you sleep. ❧ It is a time of advice with current problems and instruction to increase your knowledge of spiritual matters. ❧ There are of course Guides who have temporarily joined your group to walk with you for a special purpose. ❧ You could say they are freelance and are able to do this because they have a special knowledge. ❧ Except for your Guardian – who has been with you from your first moment in a physical body – other Guides and Helpers will come and go as the need arises."

Verse 117

Themes:
- Earth Changes
- Civilisation
- Free Will
- New Age

"If you have a house that has fallen into disrepair, then the best course of action is to pull it down and start again. ∾ In past eons of Earth time there have been civilisations that have been in decline and become beyond repair. ∾ The only way forward is to allow the destruction that must follow and start again. ∾ This has happened many times, and in each case a few were allowed to survive and become the root race for the new civilisation. ∾ You may well think that God should not allow this decline and destruction but wait – each member of each civilisation has the gift of free will. ∾ It is when this gift is used wrongly in the collective sense that nations and civilisations fall into ruin. ∾ If you misuse your gift of free will, then you and those around you will suffer *if* you take the wrong decision. ∾ At that point it is within your power to put right your mistake. ∾ This does not work in the same way when applied to whole civilisations, especially when the point of no return has been passed. ∾ This is happening to the current situation on the Earth Plane. ∾ *Too* many are exercising their free will to the detriment of others. ∾ The gift should not be used in isolation of others needs, especially when applied to whole nations. ∾ To force others to follow the whim of one or even a few is arrogance and the work of tyrants. ∾ Such actions start the decline of the civilisation and it is usually found that any spiritual understanding is in denial. ∾ When we say that the present Earth civilisation is in decline, its full effects will not be felt for some time to come, but there *will* come the destruction and the consequent rebuilding of a new way of life. ∾ The few who remain to provide the root race will be those who will lay down a strong spiritual base for the new enlightened age to come. ∾ For many years passed there have been warnings of the coming catastrophe, but no-one has been prepared to change direction or their way of living. ~ Look around and see for yourselves the greed and lust that seems to find a lodging in every corner of most nations."

This reading was given on 6th August 2000.

Verse 118

Themes:

Energy · Giving · Receiving

"All that you can see and touch is energy – ever flowing energy. All that was, and is ever created is energy. ~ That wonderful Supreme Being you know as God is infinite energy. ~ You say that nothing stays the same – it *is* ever changing – and that is because it is 'energy' which flowing, just as a river is flowing. ~ If the energy is prevented from flowing it becomes stagnant and will begin to cause trouble. ~ In the case of physical beings on the Plane of Earth it takes the form of disease. ~ Human beings *must* interact with each other in the exchange of ideas, of material help and with healing. ~ The best way to keep energy flowing as it should is to give. ~ Whatever it is *you* need, then *you* must first of all give it. ~ That may sound strange, but many will understand exactly what is meant by that. ~ For instance, if you need love because if for any reason you feel unloved then *you* must give out love. ~ We do not advise embarrassing demonstrations but mentally give love to everyone you meet. ~ As you have started the flow of love, love will flow to you in return; it must do so, it is the Natural Law. ~ When you pass someone in the street who has difficulty with walking, then send a thought of healing and the strength to cope with their condition. ~ When you give money or material goods, give with joy and a blessing. ~ Because of the energy flow, you will receive when *you* need it most. ~ You may be very good at giving, but do not forget that it is just as important to receive with as much joy as you gave. ~ If you dislike the idea of receiving and even refuse a gift, then you are blocking the flow of energy. ~ If you have nothing to give from a material sense then give a silent prayer of blessing; in many cases that is just as important as giving tangible goods. ~ Whenever you visit someone, you may wish to take a gift to show pleasure at the visit, but if you are unable to do so, remember to bless them and their household. ~ All these mental thoughts and prayers keep the energy flowing in the way it should."

Verse 119

Themes:
Conservation God Nature

"There are some people who do not believe that God exists. There are others who think that there is a God 'somewhere' out there, but other than that the whole idea is rather hazy. ~ It is perhaps because too much emphasis is placed on the possibility that God has the body of a man. ~ That is when the whole concept of a powerful being – in the body of a man – cannot be envisaged. ~ We say forget that God looks in any way like a man. ~ God is a vast energy; in fact there are no words of language that can truly describe what God is. ~ Rather than trying to place God within language, look at all that God creates out of His own Mind. ~ He has created the human form to live in a physical body. ~ Then comes all the members of the animal kingdom – from the very smallest to the largest – all with their special tasks to carry out. ~ The Plane of Earth could not continue without the animals; for as you know, each depends on the other for survival and *you* depend on them for *your* survival. ~ The vegetable kingdom is essential for the survival of the animals and birds, for without the plants and trees there would be no life on the Earth Plane. ~ There are the rocks and the soil that came from the rocks which form the basis of *all* growth. ~ All this was created by

God in whose Mind was the Plan for Life to come into being on a planet such as Earth. ~ The next time that you may doubt that God exists, look at the plants and trees and ask yourself how these could be without a Being such as God, who could create and sustain such beauty? ~ Man himself seems only able to destroy that which is beautiful; however, all is not gloomy. ~ Man is beginning to understand that Nature needs a little help, if the beauty that is, is to continue. ~ We ask you to try to ensure that you leave *your* little piece of *your* world as beautiful as you found it, when it is your time to return to Spirit."

Verse 120

Themes:
Ascension Death Life's Lessons

"The thought of reincarnation may fill many with horror; especially so, if their current experience is one of hardship, poverty or general unhappiness. ~ A large number of those on the Plane of Earth at this time will have to return to the Earth at some point in the future. ~ The reason we say this, is that it depends – at the moment of passing to our World of Spirit – what are 'the thoughts' in mind. ~ If there is any desire that is left unfulfilled, you will be drawn back to the Plane of Earth at some future time whether you like the idea now or not. ~ If your friendships or your marriage partners have not filled your needs or you have not completed theirs, then it will be necessary to return in order to do so. ~ In order to be able to leave the Earth behind and have no desires in any direction whatever, you must be able to feel you have – through your many lives – experienced all the attractions of the material and the physical. ~ Apart from this statement, we must presume that you have learned your lessons and overcome the lusts of the body; then with no desires left, you will be able to claim your place in the World of Spirit without that 'magnetic-like' pull that the Earth

Plane can exert on all its members. ❧ Those who have learned well and achieved most – as we have described – may need one more experience of the Earth vibration. ❧ It is then that an incarnating Soul just touches the Earth Plane and leaves it almost immediately. ❧ Perhaps it is necessary to stay a few years into childhood and then be taken, but *always* these child passings are for a reason. ❧ It is a 'point of understanding' that *all* are working towards. ❧ It is a point where there is an 'inner knowing' of that incredible peace when true knowledge flows into the being. ❧ It is a time when you can at last feel at one with all humanity and with all that is. ❧ You may not be aware that you have reached this point, but as soon as you come home to Spirit there will be celebration indeed."

Verse 121

Themes:
Giving Love Receiving Service

"In the lives of most people there is 'a need.' ❧ For many, the need is very pressing and it is not always about money. ❧ For some, the need is for companionship that will take away that emptiness of being alone. ❧ Others need a better place to live for themselves and their families. ❧ Those who are sick need a healing. ❧ There is a need in almost every life, but many feel that no-one is listening to them nor understanding their plight. ❧ When there is a worry that is uppermost in the mind, the ears are closed because it is felt that nothing can be done for them. ❧ Something *can* be done to break the negative pattern. ❧ You must start to do what you were placed on the Earth Plane to do; that is to serve. ❧ Unless you serve others, you cannot expect others to serve you. ❧ Another important word comes into its own here and that is love. ❧ The intended basis of every life on your Plane of Earth is love and service. ❧ Whatever *you* need, you must first of all give. ❧ If you need money, then first you must give a little to one who is in greater need, but at the same time you must give it with love and a blessing from your heart. ~ Whatever it is that you have, share it with others and not only with friends and family. ~ If you share with your friends and family only, it becomes an insurance against your possible need in the future. ~ When you share, it must be without expectation of a return. ~ If you cannot give money then give a kindness or a service. ~ Search your heart to remember any who may have hurt or caused you difficulty in the past and forgive them. ~ If you cannot forgive all hurts of the past, then you are withholding the love that God has given you to share with others. ~ Pray for all who persecute others wherever they are in your world. ~ Remember, that receiving is a part of giving; it completes the continuous circle of giving and receiving. ~ When you truly understand these things, you will find that *your* needs will be met."

Verse 122

Themes:
Unconditional Love

"We have spoken to you many times about love and we do not mean the sentimental type of love that is displayed on the Earth Plane. ~ We speak of unconditional love; love that is given without the various conditions that usually binds it around. When you were created out of God Himself, it was out of the love energy that is God Himself. ~ God is unconditional love. ~ His love He gives to every part of His Creation without question, and continues to give that love whatever the human aspect of His Creation does or says. ~ Even if you decide to dwell in the darkness of Spirit, God's love is still there for you if you were to turn to Him again. ~ From the least in the order of Creation to the Angels at the Godhead, *all* depend on His loving energy for their very being. ~ Everything has been provided for you on your Plane of Earth to learn from your various experiences in order to progress to higher levels of spiritual understanding. ☙ To help you on your way you are given 'free will' to enable you to make the best choices in order to advance your progress. ☙ Only a God of pure love could give you everything you could want and ask for so little in return. ☙ He asks that you follow His way of love towards each other. ☙ He asks that you do not judge before you offer your love, but embrace all to yourselves, because God has given you everything that you have. ☙ This also means loving your enemies. ☙ We know that it has often been said, but it remains true. ☙ In practice it means sending your loving thoughts to those who act wrongly or cause others pain. ☙ Send your thoughts to the leaders of countries who do not hold their peoples in love. ☙ We find it difficult, because of the limitations of language, to try to describe the glory and wonder of the vast energy that you call God. ☙ We are more aware of it than are you, but your understanding will grow if you will but accept that *it* is, and *you* are, because of Him. ☙ Unconditional love does not judge by wealth, appearance or creed but is given whatever happens."

Verse 123

Themes:

- Charity
- Compassion
- Tragedies
- Unconditional Love

"A picture can tell its own story and often in a most dramatic way. ☙ You see pictures that are beamed from across the Plane of Earth that tug at the heart strings. ☙ There are pictures of people in serious difficulties with their homes destroyed and no food, but it is the pictures of little children in distress, that cause you to send out your loving thoughts of healing and help, that *do indeed* bring them the help they need. ☙ Even the hardest of heart find that 'feeling' of love and compassion towards these souls welling up within themselves. ☙ Years ago, when this ability to send news and pictures in this way was as yet to be discovered, news of harrowing events was carried overland at the speed of a horse, and many months would pass before extremes of similar tragedies were known to the people at large. ❧ The impact on feelings of love and compassion were very much less than instant pictures. ❧ It helps *us* in *our* work to bring healing where it is wanted most of all, when there are large numbers sending there love at a critical time. Technical advances such as these *do* help us greatly in the work we strive to carry out. ❧ We would add that *all* thoughts of love and healing are used and receive God's blessing because they come from the heart. ❧ Those who send goods to help others in great need also receive God's blessing. ❧ It is unfortunate that there are a few who will give to a charity out of duty and think that they are doing a good deed – they are not! ❧ It would be better if they would keep their goods, until they feel that 'welling up' of compassion for others from within themselves. ❧ When this happens to them, then whatever they can give – if *only* a loving thought – it will be truly blessed. Remember, you cannot buy your place in the World of Spirit. You earn your place by the life you lead, and by the way you think and the way you treat others. ❧ It is *your* inner feelings which should govern all your actions towards other people, whoever they are, and wherever they live on the Earth Plane."

Verse 124

Themes:
- Civilisation
- Future of Planet Earth
- Humility
- Liberty

"Today, you are asked to remember those, who willingly answered the call to defend the liberty of *their* people from the tide of evil that was attempting to sweep the Plane of Earth. We would like to remind you here that it was *not* a unique event. ❧ Since the Plane of Earth was made ready for humans to live on it, there have been many similar events when the evil which prevailed at that time sounded the knell of destruction, and within a very short time *that* civilisation was destroyed. ❧ Each day *you* shape your own future by your thoughts. ❧ Collectively you can imagine how it would be possible to create 'such hatred' that those thoughts were able to destroy everything around. ❧ You may think that this is fanciful talk but we must remind you again that 'thoughts' *are* things. ❧ The more such destructive thoughts are indulged, the more likely that they will come about. ❧ It is good that *all* should remember what could have happened if those seeds of destruction – that were growing – had been allowed full growth. It would have created such hatred within the conquered peoples, that those seeds would have found fulfilment and the destruction of the Plane of Earth as you know it would have taken place. ❧ As with the fall of all civilisations, it does not happen overnight; but there *are* calamities that would take large numbers away at a time until only a few were left to make a new start. ❧ Those few would be selected and inspired to start again. ❧ In the course of many centuries, a new Earth Plane would emerge better than the previous one and taking a different path. ❧ They would be guided to keep the dark negative thoughts at bay. ❧ You have 'free will' but we try to impress upon you all the importance of right thinking. ❧ From where we are, we can see that there is a danger of destruction. ❧ There is too much emphasis on personal power and profit, and not enough thought given to those who have so much less. ❧ We would recommend a little more humility from all leaders and to include *all* in their plans."

This reading was given on 12th November 2000.

Verse 125

Themes:

- Emotional Deprivation
- Life Purpose
- Prison
- Unique Talent

"As we have often reminded you, there is no such thing as an accident. ❧ Perhaps that is difficult for some to understand, but it is true whether it fits in with your belief system or not. ~ There is a purpose behind every activity and every event. ~ You came into *your* world for a purpose. ~ It is for each one to discover what that purpose is, and to act upon it. ~ Each one has a unique talent with an ability to express that talent in a unique way. ~ There is also a particular *need* for that talent, and when the two can join forces then follows true happiness and achievement. ~ It may take the whole of your lifetime on the Earth Plane to uncover your ability. ~ Even if you have discovered your talent while still young, it may take many Earth years to find its true expression. ~ It is in the searching and seeking for your personal reason for incarnation, that the lessons of life are being learned. ~ Even when you have found your unique talent, it does not follow that the need will be there when you want it. ~ Perhaps the time is not yet right to demonstrate your gift, but that should not stop you from taking life as it comes and giving service where it is needed the most. ~ When we speak of a special talent, we do not necessarily mean something of major proportions in science or art, but the ability to do something especially well that only *you* can achieve. ~ Those who have not found their life purpose are those who are not interested in such a possibility, or those who are deprived of love or personal esteem. ~ They know from within that there is a driving force that makes them want to be noticed, and it is because they know of no life purpose or of service to others, that they cause trouble and unhappiness for others. ~ Think for a moment, if that tremendous energy that is often displayed was given to the service of others, what a wonderful transformation there would be all over this Plane of Earth. ~ Even the youngest of children should be encouraged to find for themselves what they are best fitted for *and* be allowed to do it. ~ Much of the world's trouble is caused through inner frustration. ~ Ask for God's help in showing that there is a better way of love and peace."

Verse 126

Themes:
- Change
- Incarnation
- Free Will
- Spiritual Growth

"We are travellers on a cosmic journey; a journey that will last forever. ~ For, as we have often said, 'We are eternal beings that *must* accept change as the journey progresses.' ~ The 'I' – the Ego – has always existed, but for many ages slept within arms of the Creator before being sent forth as an individual being to claim that 'I'. ~ It was *then* we realised, that we had been given the means to decide for ourselves – with the gift of free choice – how we should conduct our lives. ~ It is now that we also understand that there is a limitation on that free choice, in that it must be governed by the initial framework that is laid down for each one before incarnation into the World of Matter. ~ That limitation is essential for our well being; for if we had absolutely free choice in every sense of the word, it would lead to chaos in a very short time. ~ We occupy the World of Matter for so brief a period that to bring the greatest benefit, change must walk with us at all times. ~ This can be disruptive from a purely personal point of view but necessary to achieve spiritual development. ~ It is this development that is the reason for each incarnation. ~ The experiences and the changes we face from day to day, bring to each one the glimmers of understanding that we need to take the next step on the pathway of life. ~ So often we hear the cry go up after an Earthly tragedy: 'Why does God allow this to happen? And, there *cannot* be a God if such terrible things are allowed to take place.' ~ If you are tempted to say similar words, remember, *you* have free choice and if God stepped in and prevented those events, then the gift He gave you would have been taken away. ~ The *world* chooses how to act, and if a very unpleasant way is chosen then that is how it must be. ~ However tragic the circumstance, the time to leave the Earth

Plane is already laid down and it does not matter whether that one is young or old. ↜ When that time comes to depart, free choice ends."

Verse 127

Themes:

Christmas Goodwill

"You are fast approaching a time of present giving and merry making. ↜ That is good for all those who are able to take part. ↜ There is a feeling of goodwill towards most, if not all the people. ↜ We ask, 'Why is that feeling of goodwill to others to be reserved for a few days around that period? ↜ Why is it not possible to make that effort every day?' ↜ We also have *our* own celebrations at this time. ↜ For us, it a time to listen to those who visit from the Higher Spheres and enjoy the strength and courage they bring with them. ↜ The instruction and challenges they bring with them is invaluable for the work we undertake on their behalf. ↜ It is becoming more obvious that the underlying meaning of this festival is lost to most people, and it has been taken over by those who can see a way to make large profits for themselves. ↜ If you cannot accept the reason for *this* festival, make it a season to remember those who have little of the world's goods, and endeavour to make their lives more comfortable. ↜ It is not only the poorer countries of the world who need your thoughts but those who are nearer your own homes who are also in need. ↜ There are those who have no shelter, little food, and certainly no warmth when the weather is cold and they are sick. ↜ We know there are many problems to overcome in order to help these sad people, but your prayers *will* help them, especially when those prayers are sent with love. ↜ Know that your prayers are powerful indeed for they can bring benefit to those in need where money alone cannot. ↜ Feel that goodwill every day of the year. ↜ It matters not whether you follow a particular path, for that is personal choice; but loving all God's creation is an essential part of spiritual growth. ~ Let the seed of peace and love grow within each one and let it spread throughout the Plane of Earth. ~ In ancient times when the light of day was at its shortest, the people were afraid that the sun might disappear altogether and so they lit fires and made merry to encourage the sun to come back and lengthen the days again. ~ You can celebrate knowing that the sun will rise again tomorrow."

Verse 128

Themes:

- Appearance
- Designer Clothes
- Initial Impressions
- Judging Others

"It is unfortunate that *your* part of your world is becoming more judgemental with regards to others. ~ There has always been a 'flash of judgement' when meeting another for the first time. ~ In the past it was where you came from, because of your accent or your religion. ~ The type and quality of clothing also played a part, but often it was the grooming of the individual that was so important. ~ There has *always* been some form of judgement on meeting another person. ~ Now we observe that not only is all this still true, but a new dimension has crept in. ~ It is not only the clothes but the maker or name on those clothes. ~ We cannot understand why so much importance is placed on these things. ~ When we come into contact with those of the Earth Plane we take no notice of the outer covering but the quality – or otherwise – of what is underneath. ~ In other words we see the real person. We see what they are, what it is they are trying to achieve, and the distance they have travelled down the path of spiritual understanding. ~ On first meeting you will of course see the outer cover, but it is unwise to form any kind of judgement of that person until you know them rather better. ~ Your saying of not judging a book by its cover applies here. ~ In fact, there should not be any kind of judgement applied by anyone to another, but that is almost impossible to achieve in the kind of world *you* live in. ~ We hope that you will look for the 'real person' underneath the external trappings. ~ This will take a little time, for there are few who will display all of their private nature on first meeting; but there are others where it is quite obvious that caution should be applied to any dealings with them. ~ When you find that you must in any way judge another's character, we urge you to be kind in your thoughts and offer a silent prayer for that soul; that *they* may find a spiritual vein in *their* dealings with others. ~ All on the Earth Plane can aim higher, and it is for this reason that we come to inspire and help where we can."

Verse 129

Themes:
- Greed
- Power
- Unconditional Love
- War

"As we have often said, God is not a grand old man sitting in the Heavens, as many still believe when they think of God. ~ It is not possible to describe God in any language, for God is a vast, all embracing energy of love. ~ That wondrous energy has created all that is, from the greatest to the very smallest. Everything is of Spirit. ~ All that comes under the name of Nature, from the smallest leaf to the greatest tree; every animal, bird and insect was created by God out of that well of love. ~ All peoples are Spirit; whether on the Plane of Earth or living on the many other worlds that exist. ~ They were created individuals in their own right out of that love which is God. ~ Everyone is a brother or sister to the other, and should offer this love no matter what may have been done. ~ This uncon–ditional love must be given without regard to race, colour of skin or the religion of that person. ~ You may not like their activities, but in times of need or persecution, you must offer help in whichever way you can. ~ The help can take many forms, from sending physical help, food and medicines or your healing prayers. ~ There is a great deal of help that is sent every day to those in need. ~ It is *these* actions, which is an expression of unconditional love, that we have described. ~ If the whole world *did* understand this love, then the suffering of the masses of people would stop; war would end and peace would begin. ~ This does not mean that the tensions would cease but that peaceful tolerance would take hold. ~ Those with warlike ideas would not learn to love their enemies, but would begin to see that fighting wins little and that peaceful discussion is likely to yield a better result. ~ In the course of many years yet to come this *will* happen. ~ All the while that 'power' is the corrupting factor and the wealth that comes from it holds sway, then there is no reason for them to change what already exists. ~ Each one can make a difference by sending out thoughts of peace and healing for others in the world who are in great need."

Verse 130

Themes:
- Forgiveness

"As a human being, there is one important attribute that we wish to bring to notice since little enough is said about 'forgiveness'. ~ To really understand the human condition, it is necessary to be able to forgive. ~ We know that it *does* depend on the depth of forgiveness that is required, as to whether the desired forgiveness is forthcoming. ~ It may be easy to forgive someone who has said something unkind, either to you or about you to another. ~ It may be very different to instantly offer forgiveness to one who has maligned you, in such a way that it leads to a loss of livelihood and all that it entails. ~ If there is an element of truth in what has been said about you, even if there has been exaggeration, then it will require some soul searching and an inward promise to do better next time. ❧ It is often said that there is no smoke without fire, and it is a lesson to be understood that one's life should be conducted in such a way as to *not* attract adverse comment and exaggeration. ❧ We know how difficult it is to lead a life that is entirely pure or honourable, but before starting again, as one is urged to do, it is wise to start with a clean sheet and offer forgiveness to those who have hurt you deeply. ❧ It is not necessary to go to them and offer your forgiveness, but to enter the silence and offer it from deep within your heart. ❧ If you do *not* do this, you will be in bondage to those who have hurt you. ❧ Whatever the hurt, and we know the anguish that can be caused by others, then the only way to free yourself from them is to offer that forgiveness. ❧ We know it is very difficult to accomplish, but you must try. ❧ Remember to ask for Spirit's help when you try to forgive, and if you are sincere, you will succeed. ❧ You will know that you have done this noble thing when you feel a weight fall from your shoulders and find the freedom that *you* have given to another. ❧ You will have taken another step on the spiritual pathway."

Verse 131

Themes:
Death Joy Spiritualism Truth

"When you all meet together at times such as this, it should be an occasion of joy and laughter – when appropriate of course. At the same time is it also one of serious note. ❧ We bring you truth, which must be taken seriously as no doubt you will agree; but we also try to lift the vibrations by inspiration in the address, and sometimes it is possible in bringing your loved ones to you by demonstrating some earthly mannerism and such like. ❧ However our words and descriptions come to you, they bring you truth; truth that you *never* die but simply change your rate of vibration to a much higher level. ❧ This means that you have to leave your earthly body behind, and live a different life in another dimension. ❧ Most of you will have visited that 'other dimension' during your sleep state *and* met your loved ones, but only realise that something 'different' has happened and you 'think' it a dream. ❧ All this sounds like serious business and it is, but with knowledge such as this, you can live your lives on the Plane of Earth with a greater sense of freedom and happiness. ❧ You know that your loved ones are free of their pain and you know that any distress you suffer at the end of your life is cured at the moment of passing to the higher state of living. ❧ That in itself should give you a sense of joy. ❧ With this knowledge you can achieve a sense of balance in the physical life, which is so denied those who cling to the belief that death is the end of everything. ❧ People who do think this way dread getting older and closer to that fearful day, and this alone colours all that they think and do. ❧ We know of the wonderful feeling of release when they discover that life is indeed eternal. ❧ We want you to ensure that *your* life is in balance with the knowledge that you have and with this 'truth' as your anchor, the more 'down to earth' feeling of joy it will bring. ❧ Knowing that you are a part of the Father of Creation and that your Father will hear your prayers in your time of need, should bring that ripple of happiness."

Verse 132

Themes:
Death Ghosts Lost Spirits

"There has been reference to 'lost Souls' and 'earthbound Spirits' but no explanation has been offered as to what this means. ❧ First of all a Soul or Spirit cannot be lost. ❧ Your Father, Creator of all that is, knows everything concerning His creation. ❧ There is great confusion in the minds of many about what happens – if anything – after death. ❧ For many people death is the end, for this is what they have been taught. When the moment of death arrives, as it will for every Soul on the Plane of Earth, they find that they are *still* alive. ❧ This is when the fog of confusion descends. ❧ Those in the World of Spirit draw close to that Soul to offer guidance and help, but they are rebuffed. ❧ Many times great effort is made to explain that 'wrong' information has been given to them while they were on Earth. ❧ Sometimes their loved ones are brought to them to help with their understanding, but they will not listen because they think it a form of trickery. ❧ They are left to wander with Spirit Helpers always on hand, should that Soul change their mind. ❧ Those that are termed 'earthbound' want to hold onto the pleasures of Earth that they know, and refuse to accept that there is a world more wonderful in every way than the Earth could offer. ❧ They think that if they give up their hold on the Earth they will lose everything they have ever loved. ❧ In the case of hauntings, those Souls are held to places of former misery and it is an expression of revenge for their suffering. ❧ Remember, they cannot move onto their proper place in the World of Spirit until they trust their Helpers to lead them to their loved ones and a place of safety in the World of Spirit. ❧ Eventually these Souls will listen, and allow their Helpers to lead them to a wonderful land of beauty and peace. ❧ Some will wander – apparently lost – for a long time, but they will not be aware of that since there is no time in Spirit. ❧ Even under these conditions they are protected and safe."

Verse 133

Themes:
- Life Purpose
- Soul Purpose

"There are two questions often asked. ❧ The first seems to be: 'Why am I here?' and the second, 'Who am I?' ❧ The reason you are on the Plane of Earth is to learn from each other and from the general experiences of the life being lived. ☙ Each one is at a different level of understanding, and it is because you are all together in no particular order that you learn from each other. ☙ Some will say that learning could be done equally as well in the World of Spirit but we disagree. When you are called home to Spirit, you are drawn to those of the same level of spiritual understanding and experience; therefore, you would not be in a position to learn from each other in the same way. ☙ On the Earth Plane you have no option but to experience the ways of others *and* their misunderstandings or lack of any belief in anything but themselves. ☙ You come up against their selfish ways with no feeling for compassion for the suffering of others. ☙ In the World of Spirit you would have to be determined to find those who felt this way. ☙ There are many of course, but if it were *not* of your nature, you would have to look for it. ☙ The God of all Wisdom knows that the ways of Earth teach all that is needed to become a perfect human being. ☙ This will take many many lives, but the 'Crown of Perfection' is the greatest achievement for all spiritual beings. ☙ There are other worlds with beings striving along the same paths of learning as are you; all are working and serving each other to attain this highest accolade. ☙ No-one knows how long this will take but does it matter – you have all eternity! ☙ To the question: 'Who am I?' ☙ You should know the answer to that question since God created each one out of Himself. ☙ At *that* moment each one was perfect, but you did not know you were perfect. ☙ In order to serve the needs of Creation that perfection had to be tempered with knowledge and experience. ☙ From that moment, life on the World of Matter had begun and the concepts of love and compassion were being understood."

Verse 134

Themes:

♨ Unconditional Love

"There are many sayings on the Earth Plane about love. ❧ For instance, you say that, 'love makes the world go round' and another that, 'love is everything.' ❧ If you truly believe that, why is it that so much seems to be demonstrated against love? We think it is that very few on the Plane of Earth know what real love is. ❧ It is definitely not sentimental love, the type written about in books or in the latest song. ❧ True love is entirely unselfish; it springs into action without thought of personal comfort or convenience. ❧ There are *many* recorded instances where there is a risk that the Earth life could be shortened because of the action of pure love; under these conditions there is no time to consider personal safety. ❧ We are not suggesting that you should take unnecessary risks in order to demonstrate your love for others; we are simply trying to indicate when unconditional love can be seen. ❧ God created *all* that is, out of pure unconditional love. ❧ There were no strings attached as to what would happen if it was not understood. ❧ True love is of the Spirit; it is a quality all its own, and is understood by others of spiritual knowledge. ❧ To many, the Earth Plane will seem a cruel and uncaring place, but to others it offers so many opportunities for learning and sharing that to them, it is a wonderful place. ❧ For those who do accept that life on the Earth is a rewarding experience they are fulfilling the reason for their incarnation. ❧ There will be difficulties of course, but you will learn and understand a little of the love that God has shown by creating *all* that is on all the Planes of Spirit and the many Worlds of Matter. ❧ You are only a tiny portion of your whole real self and your 'real self' has the greater understanding; but to the forefront of all that you have experienced, is the lesson of unconditional love. ❧ When this is accepted and understood then eternal life has a deeper meaning. ǀ All your thoughts should be illuminated by this quality of love and your actions will follow in the same manner. There is no need to boast of it because – at last – all will be known."

Verse 135

Themes:
Karma* Life Review† Passing Over

"When the time comes for you to return to Spirit, you are met by all your friends and members of your family who have gone before you. It is a reunion of the greatest happiness and joy. Its joy far outweighs any celebration that the Earth can offer. There are no misunderstandings or petty feuds because the World of Spirit can only offer love. After this gathering, you will be asked to face a review of your Earth life. To make the progress that you wish, such a review is necessary so that any debts you may owe to others can be repaid. You are not compelled to do this because of the gift of free will. You may hesitate, remembering some things you *may* not want to recall. In those moments of hesitation you will find those friends and family – who gave you such a welcome – will draw back. A decision *has* to be made, and with encouragement from your Helpers – who are still with you at this point – you decide that you will submit to this review of your life. Much will have been forgotten but *everything* is seen, whether good or not so good, of every thought and every action and how others were affected. It is rather like dropping a pebble in a pond and the ripples spreading wider and wider. Your reaction is most important. Where there is true humility much is forgiven and a bias to the good will help to compensate for the debts owed to others. However long ago the debts to others were incurred, they must be repaid in some form of service.

* Karma is the repayment of debts accrued during one's earthly lifetime.
† This review of your life takes place in what is often termed, 'The Hall of Mirrors.'

Sometimes it is possible to meet those you have offended and then forgiveness can be asked for in giving a service to another that *they* may choose. ❧ It is all a matter of putting the record straight. If you are one of the few who will not submit to this examination then there can be no progress and the future is one of isolation from all those you love, for you will not be able to mix with those who are giving service to Spirit. ❧ *All* are called to give service for God's Plan of Creation."

Verse 136

Themes:
Conflict Peace War

"So often we have brought the word peace to the fore, because it is on the minds of most people at this time. ❧ The question that many ask is: 'Why cannot the leaders find peace?' ❧ One reason for this is fear. ❧ Each side – in *any* conflict – fear that in order to have the peace that each wants that something will have to be given up. ❧ In doing this they fear that their own power will be lost. ❧ *We say* that if the need for peace is genuine, then each will be willing to give a little, in order to gain much. ❧ Here we wish to say that peace is not only the absence of something. ❧ It may be the absence of war or conflict but it is much more. ❧ Peace is an attitude of mind; it is also a position of trusting each other to abide by the terms agreed. ❧ Peace can be the absence of noise; but without understanding the adverse effect that the continuous noise is having on others, it will happen again. ❧ To achieve peace each must be willing to know what peace is. ❧ It is a combination of trust, attitude, and understanding the needs of others in relation to the self. ❧ This does not only apply when warring sides are trying to negotiate a peace settlement, but in *your* own life. ❧ Your own affairs should be conducted in a peaceful manner, and where there is disagreement, there should be quiet discussion in order to resolve the matter.

Heated arguments can only lead to mistrust and eventually even hostility between friends. ❧ Remember each one is created as a unique example of God's love for all his children. ❧ There are no two people exactly the same, so it is not surprising that there are disagreements among them from time to time. ❧ This is where unconditioned love comes to the fore and claims a position in any peace settlement. ❧ All should pray for peace but in so doing, make sure that thoughts and actions are always as peaceful as humanly possible. ❧ Make a practice every day in sending healing love out across the Earth Plane. ❧ In so doing, you will be helping to create the peace that everyone wishes to see."

This reading was given on 22nd April 2001

Verse 137

Themes:

- Building the Pyramids
- Energy
- Power of Thought

"Everything is a demonstration of energy. ❧ The Supreme Being we know as God, is the vast energy from which all else is made manifest. ❧ The differences between each human being are due to the change of vibration at which the energy is moving. ❧ It is almost impossible to attempt to describe what a 'spiritual understanding' in terms of matter is; energy is constantly on the move and because of it, matter is always changing. ❧ If this was not so there would be no wonder for the human race to try to understand. ❧ In everything you do you manipulate energy, even if the result is ugly. ❧ The artist is not usually aware that in creating a figure in perhaps wood or clay, the vibration is also being changed in order to appear as the artist had seen it in thought. ❧ Thought is the first step to any action, and the quality of the thought will decide the quality of the result. ❧ So often you have read or heard said that 'thoughts' are things. ❧ In ancient times, when true accounts are very sketchy and often quite inaccurate, there was a greater understanding of the power of thought and the potential that its use could bring. ~ At that time, there was understanding of how the vibration of energy could be used to affect matter through the power of thought. ~ Deep understanding of the processes of creating huge structures were in the hands of a select few who had studied these things. It was through this detailed knowledge that the pyramids were built. ~ To do this, it was necessary to have large numbers of people to do the base work of bringing the materials to the site for the structure to be started. ~ It was when huge stones were required to be lifted into place accurately, that the services of these specialists were brought to bear. ~ They were able to guide the many workers to the right spot and their concerted power of thought acted like heavy lifting gear to place each huge block in exactly the right place. ~ These specialists were the huge cranes you have in your world today. ~ The workers needed these thinkers, and the thinkers needed the workers to enable the work to be completed. ~ We think it is as well that such knowledge is now lost."

Verse 138

Themes:

- Greater Self
- Intuition
- Karma
- Spiritual Law
- Thoughts

"As we have said before, the immutable Laws of Spirit must *not* be broken. ~ These laws apply to all Creation throughout all planes of conscience. ~ If these laws are broken there must be repayment as in the Law of Cause and Effect. ~ There is no excuse that ignorance was the cause of breaking the law, it applies, and there must be repayment. ~ Sometimes this law is known as Karma. ~ To avoid pain and so called 'bad luck' it should be realised that most cause and effect comes into operation through the choices of small things. ~ In almost every moment, a choice is being made and most is made automatically without thought. ❧ When it is realised that this is an almost continuous activity, then it can be understood why life on the physical plane seems to go wrong more often than go right. ❧ To combat this, we advise that a careful watch is placed on *all* thoughts. ❧ We agree that this is not easy, but if you want to break the habit of long standing, a real effort must be made. ❧ When a choice presents itself, even over the smallest matter, ask yourself: 'Will this be beneficial to me and will it hurt anyone else?' ❧ If you are sure that all is well, make the choice for yourself. ❧ If however, you feel the answer is no, then do *not* make that choice. ❧ It made be hard and long winded but if you wish to make the right choices in the important issues, then you must have overcome the automatic responses over the little things. ❧ If you are ever in doubt about making the right choice – that *does* bring the Law into effect with a vengeance – then you must ask your 'inner self.' ❧ Practice doing this over the small choices – as we have outlined – then you will have confidence in receiving the right answer. ❧ If the choice you are about to make feels right in your heart then it will be right for you. ❧ You must be honest with yourself and be willing to say 'NO' to the choice on offer – however much you want it – as *your* future and personal prosperity will depend on it."

Verse 139

Themes:

- Compassion
- Poverty
- Service
- Tolerance
- Understanding

"In your world there is frequent reference to poverty and almost always this means 'a lack' – usually a lack of money. ❧ However, there are many other situations that can be classed as poverty. ❧ There is poverty of tolerance, of understanding and of compassion. ❧ These should cause as much concern as does the lack of money. ❧ The lack of money does not always cause unhappiness, whereas a lack of tolerance, understanding and compassion can be very hurtful and will cause distress. ❧ *All* this begins with thought. ❧ If your thinking is in tune with others and their conditions, then you will have the necessary compassion to help put things right. ❧ Here we must emphasise that 'more money' will not bring happiness. ❧ It is not that 'more of these' will solve all the problems, but how they are used. ❧ Much more money could make a difficult situation even worse because the recipient may not know how to use it wisely. ❧ In such a situation perhaps a little at a time would be of greater benefit. ❧ However, much more understanding, compassion and tolerance would bring light into the lives of those who have known only of being pushed into the margins of society. ❧ It is 'right thinking' and how to bring that thinking into reality for the benefit of others, that is the point of progress of those who are called to serve. There has to be an inner desire to see where help is needed and to bring that help without fanfare or fuss. ❧ This is the 'right' use of tolerance and compassion with understanding. ❧ One size does not fit all, and 'the needs' of those you wish to help *must* be taken into account, or there will be more harm done than is warranted. ❧ Then that help is termed interference! The underlying quality must be love, for no help can be true help without love. ❧ Listen to those who inspire you and you will be guided along the right path. ❧ The path of service is a long and hard one and it will bring tears of frustration as well as tears of joy, but it is the way of progress for all."

Verse 140

Themes:

♨ Forgiveness

"Your world is beset by many problems which are difficult to solve to everyone's satisfaction. ❧ Each one also has problems; some are minor, while others take longer to understand before a solution can be found. ❧ When another hurts you, there is almost always an instinctive feeling to do the same to that one, to let them know how it feels. ❧ This is not the way, as you will – on reflection – agree. ❧ If an apology is not forthcoming, then the only way is 'to forgive' the one who caused the hurt. ❧ This makes it sound unreal but think about it. ❧ If you do not forgive the one who hurt you, you will be in mental bondage to them. ❧ The hurt will always be there at the back of your thinking. ❧ In the course of an Earth lifetime there will be many hurts caused by others, which may not have been resolved. ❧ There will be the tendency to go over these hurts many times over, causing distress. ❧ As time passes, these hurts tend to grow in the imagination and before long, all mental strength and activity will be taken up by these hurts. ❧ We are setting an extreme example but we want you to understand just what could happen if you do not open your heart and forgive. ❧ First of all, realise that a soul that *is* evolved would not behave in that way; so that means they need help and understanding. ❧ Then realise, the one who hurt may have caused it at a time of personal distress and did not know how the 'sharp words' caused pain. ❧ Whatever the reason, forgive. ❧ It is easy with the help of Spirit – meditate upon it. ❧ Think of all those you must forgive – one by one – and bless them; mentally see the slate being wiped clean. ❧ On next meeting greet them with a smile, for there is no need to make any comment upon what it is that you have done. ❧ The difference will be in *your* outlook. ❧ You will feel lighter, as though a burden has been lifted from your shoulders, which of course it has. It does not mean that the incidents have been erased from your mind. ~ You *could* remember if you wished to do so, but 'it' will be in the past and your thoughts will be directed towards the future with a sense of freedom."

Verse 141

Themes:
- Change
- Connecting with Spirit
- New Year
- Time

"As you should be aware by now, we do not measure time in the same way as you. ~ This has *always* been something that you do not seem to understand. ~ You measure the passing of time by the turning of the Earth, which gives you day and night, weeks, months and years. ~ There is *no* night in the World of Spirit, so time cannot be measured in the same way. ~ We *do* have a sort of time which is measured by progress in any of the activities which we have undertaken. ~ Sometimes we are asked to advise on Earth events, but although we do try to pinpoint when a major change is likely to take place, we cannot be sure that our estimates are in any way accurate. ~ Although we are in daily contact with Earth, we do not have the same awareness of time as when *we* were an inhabitant of the Earth Plane. ~ We hope that will in some way, answer the question of timing when we are asked for advice. ~ Now that you have reached the end of another Earth year, you all wish each other a Happy New Year. ~ Some will be nervous as to the tidings that the New Year will bring, but others will welcome any change, believing that it must be better than that which they have had during the previous year. ~ We agree that change is good because it stimulates the mind, and the 'challenge of change' usually brings out the best in people. When you are faced with any change it often brings the feeling of uncertainty and the Earth mind does not like uncertainty. Remember that we are ever here to bring you strength and courage – as well as advice – if first you will ask, and having asked, be *still* and listen for the answer. ❧ Rushing about – as is the usual habit – brings noise and confusion. ❧ It is in the stillness that the small voice of Spirit will be heard. ❧ God knows every least nuance of your life since He created you. Draw close to Him and let Him bring the best New Year for your needs. ❧ Remember too to thank Him for bringing you to this day in safety and in Love."

Verse 142

Themes:

Creation · God · Love

"Each time we come to you we bring to you God's love in its many different forms. ❧ The Universe came into being because God is Love. ❧ Just as there is nothing outside of God, so there is nothing outside of love. ❧ We agree that often it is completely hidden, but that is not due to any decision or activity of God. ❧ When love is hidden it is due to human non-acceptance and disbelief. ❧ When you find it difficult to find love in general in the world, look to the birds. ❧ In the Spring they follow the urge to multiply. ❧ They do not have free will as do you, but must follow the path laid down for them. ❧ They build a nest for the warmth and safety of their young; but *have* you ever looked at the nest that is built year after year? ❧ Each species of bird knows the type of nest that is required. ❧ The correct pattern is within the bird, placed there by God's wisdom. ❧ The nest is a most intricate piece of creation; it is carefully built with the love that is within the bird. ❧ The bird does not question the love that is within it; it knows that it is supported and cared for by the Higher Realms. ❧ Each wild creature will build a suitable nest for its offspring. ❧ Each is built with the love of its Creator and this is shown by the care and beauty of its construction. ❧ It is good to question the truth of all that is, but there is so much that is offered that is truth itself. ~ Many human beings still refuse to accept that *all* is made manifest, yet God Himself brought it forth out of Love. ~ Many pray for healing and hope that they will be favoured but, is it realised that 'healing itself' is the highest form of love to be shown on the Earth Plane? ~ For all the latest inventions that come into being, few will accept that it is so because of God's continuing love for all His creation. ~ God knows nothing of evil acts, cruelty or greed for the material. ~ Those things are entirely the responsibility of those concerned; God is pure love and knows nothing outside of Love."

Appendices

Appendix – Note 1.

Astrology   Incarnation   Natal Chart
Time and Date of Birth

(Verses: 48 and 49)

Appendix – Note 2.

Personal Power

(Verses: 44, 69, 70)

Appendix – Note 3.

Natural / Spiritual Laws

(Verses: 20, 34, 72, 84, 93)

Appendix – Note 4.

God – the Ultimate Being

Appendix – Note 1.

Astrology – Natal Chart – Time and Date of Birth

In the coming years mankind will raise its vibration, and in so doing become the Spiritual People that they were always meant to be. They will understand that their Earth Life was planned and that they were part of the planning. The Wise Ones in the World of Spirit decide what time and date the baby will be born to attract the correct influences of Planets and Stars that will help that soul on his or her life journey.

There are already Astrologers who, if given your exact time, date and place of birth, will be able to tell you why you incarnated at this time and what you have arrived upon Earth to learn during your lifetime.

The exact time, place and date of birth is one of the greatest gifts a parent can give to their children.

Tishelle Betterman is one such great Astrologer and can be found on www.astrolady.com

Appendix – Note 2.

Personal Power

It may seem strange, but mankind in the 21st Century, is possibly at its lowest point spiritually, than at any other time during the last 3,000 years.

Spirit took over from here:

> "Yesteryear, we in the World of Spirit chose not to teach the new generations the wisdoms of the past. Greed, anarchy and hated typify today's society, but in the future – sometime in the not too distant future – the upcoming generations will be given once again, the power of choice to include celestial wisdoms as part of everyday life; and in so doing the powers that mankind of generations past once knew, will once again be given: the Wisdoms from the World of Spirit. There is no better time on the Earth Plane than now, to create the Stepping Stones towards mankind's future and the future of the Planet Earth. In this book lie all that is needed at this time of mankind's development."

Appendix – Note 3.

Natural / Spiritual Laws

Spirit took over from here:

> "Not too long ago we started a journey that will elevate mankind to his rightful place; that place is to be a part of the World of Nature; for he is but one part of many. The birds and animals, the plants and trees and the wonderful life that fill the oceans of the world are the other parts that we speak of. The Master Maitreya bought to you the New Teachings from our World. They are brought at a time in mankind's evolutionary cycle when he/she needs to realign themselves with the Creator of all the Universe – the energy that you call God. If only you will take the time to read this wonderful and exciting revelation then you too will have started that journey – the wonderful journey of life and the teachings of the soul."

Maitreya ISBN 0-9548959-1-6

Appendix – Note 4.

In all these texts God is referred to as He or Him. It should be noted that God is an infinite energy and as such is both male and female.

There is no distinction between male and female since both are totally equal; even though they perform different functions on the Earth Plane.

Guidance Notes for:

**Philosophers, Theologians,
Archaeologists and Research Students.**

While most people understand the nature of Metaphysics, this may be your first introduction to the fact that there are many people in the world today – in the 21st Century – who talk to Spirit on a day to day basis. ❧ There is absolutely nothing new in this. ❧ Over the centuries Prophets, Medicine Men, Shamans, Sages, Avatars, Witches, Heretics, Wise Men and today's Mediums and Channels have all been given messages from Spirit to pass onto their fellow man. ❧ After all this time the majority still fear and choose not to listen. ❧ Fortunately the days of the Salem Witches and the burning of Joan of Arc – all Mediums – are over.

This book offers a unique opportunity to study and to learn things that are true and have that elevated quality of integrity and honesty.

Verses 44, 45, 117 and 137 are spectacular starting points for reflecting upon everything you know and have to date held as *your* truth.

Should you require any further help, guidance or a speaker presentation, please contact the Author or Publisher through:

Kevin Brookes
Spiritual Philosophy Publishing Limited
PO Box 79,
Midhurst
West Sussex
GU29 9WW

www.spiritualphilosophy.co.uk

The New Spiritual Laws

Maitreya
Teachings from Heaven
– Volume 1 –

The Book:

Spirit took over from here:

"Once, many moons ago in the cycle of the Planet Earth a Master was born, his name was Yeshua or Jesus as you know him in the West. He was a great Master and still is. He was brought to Earth to teach mankind the meaning of Unconditional Love; something that the generations who read this text no longer know about. Time and politics have eroded the true meaning of God – the Creator of all that is in the Universes, yours and the many beyond. Once again we come to teach mankind the true Laws of Spirit. It is within the Teachings of the Master Maitreya that the wisdoms have been given again in a form that mankind can understand in the 21st Century. In eons to come, we will come again talking in the languages of the future, as yet unwritten. Now it is time to listen once again and to learn as you were always meant to do. But this time do it for yourself; do it for your children; do it for their future and once that is achieved, then mankind will – once again –be at peace with themselves and the beautiful World of Nature of which they are just one tiny part."

ISBN 0-9548959-1-6

The perfect book to begin your Spiritual Journey

Some Silent Hero

The Book:

Vivien Goddard is a young woman in her 20s with no idea where she wants to go or what she wants to do with her life. Struggling to come to terms with the death of her father and the drudgery of life with her alcoholic mother, she fails her 'A' Levels. Viv sees no way out until a chance visit to the local Spiritualist Church, with her friend Rena, starts a whirlwind of synchronicities and amazing happenings. David, a mysterious biker befriends her and together they wend their way to the West Coast of America accompanied by a little girl from the World of Spirit. This inspirational tale delves into the very real world of Spirit Guides and Guardian Angels but with a refreshing approach that leaves the reader inspired and wanting to create their very own spiritual journey.

Author:

Stephanie Brookes, at 24 years, is probably one of the youngest writers in the Mind, Body & Spirit genre. She finished the script one day after her graduation ceremony at Portsmouth University in July 2004. She aims to travel and live on the West Coast of America & Canada to research and write the second book, 'The Chief's Forgotten Land,' in 2006.

ISBN 0-9548959-0-8

Look out for our upcoming titles:

Sequel to "Some Silent Hero"

"The Chief's Forgotten Land"
Stephanie Brookes

Vivian has changed; she has a newfound belief in herself. While her family want her to return home to England, her guide assures her that, at this point in time, she might wish to stay in America. Synchronicity and a compelling urge to experience the ancient wisdoms of the North American Indian tribes lead her north to the lands of the giant Redwoods. Here she meets a Shaman who tells her he has been waiting many, many years for her to come to him.

****

A UK and World Debut:

"Maitreya"
Messages from the Master
Volume II
Channelled by Margaret Birkin.

In Volume I, Maitreya gave us his teachings to help mankind rediscover its connection with the Divine Spirit, God. In Margaret's second book, Maitreya gives us guidance to help each one of us in our daily lives. He talks about the human conditions, creating abundance, eliminating world poverty, education, business, religion, sexual repression, stem cells, abortion, love, world peace and simply having fun. All of the messages are given to uplift and encourage. There is nothing of the negative only of the positive. It *will* change the lives of everyone that reads it.

****

Index

C.

D.

E.

F.

G.

H.

I.

M.

N.

O.

P.

R.

S.

T.

U.

V.

W.

Y.

Author's Profile:

Désirée Jestico

Désirée was born in Pulham St Mary, Norfolk. She joined the WAAF in 1942 and served in the Meteorological Office; staying as a civilian after demob in 1946 before transferring to Victory House, Kingsway, London to the young ladies on the Ministry roof! She married, had a son and was widowed in 1996. It was after this time that she studied to become a Healer and shortly after began receiving these inspired readings. She is a remarkable lady of 81 years of age.